BUSINESS ETHICS
IN A CHANGING CULTURE

BUSINESS ETHICS IN A CHANGING CULTURE

Richard C. Chewning

E. Claiborne Robins School of Business
University of Richmond

Reston Publishing Co., Inc.
A Prentice-Hall Company
Reston, Virginia

Dedicated to

DR. FRANCIS A. SCHAEFFER
—to the author, a Barnabas—

ISBN 0-8359-0566-7
Library of Congress Catalog No. 82-74194

PRINTED IN THE UNITED STATES OF AMERICA
10 9 8 7 6 5 4 3 2 1

Designed and typeset by Publications Development Co. of
Crockett, Texas, Developmental Editor: Nancy Marcus Land,
Production Associate: Janice Turner

PREFACE

We are living in an ethically schizophrenic society. That is, a society which is unable to agree internally on what is "right" or "wrong" when decisions must be made that affect the whole body. Because of this inability to develop an ethical consensus, we manifest basic disagreements that cause us to think ill of one another when we are on opposite sides of important issues such as: distribution of our wealth; conservation of our environment; protection of human health; definition of our rights; and many other economic/social problems. It is demonstrably clear that our different ethical values lie at the very heart of our inability to find reconcilable solutions to the problems.

Ethical schizophrenia is not, however, to be confused with *pluralism*. For over two hundred years our society exhibited an amazing ability to both absorb and/or let stand alone the diverse religious, racial, ethnic, and social groups. These bodies could maintain a particular identity associated with their heritage or join the larger corpus and gain their identity by functioning within the broader society. This has been called *pluralism*. During this same period of time, however, there was a broad ethical consensus about what was right and wrong which reflected our basic beliefs flowing from our Judaic/Christian heritage. Pluralism reflected our diverse heritages and aspirations, but underneath these vast differences was the broadly accepted ethical framework that was capable of producing a consensus on the basic assumptions concerning the desired character for the society—private property, individualism, etc. The old consensus has been shattered, however. A new one has not yet emerged. We are in internal conflict. Contradictions and confusion are now "normal." Culturally, we are ethically schizophrenic.

The establishment of our historic ethic, and the forces that emerged to shatter its grip on us, are set forth in very broad and general terms to enable the reader to gain perspective. The force and consequences of this conflict are enormous. In many ways it is like a cultural divorce. We are being ripped apart. Our very identity is threatened. Portraying this great struggle between such enormous forces in such broad and sweeping terms is also the Achilles heel of the work. Scholars who have devoted their lives to the study of philosophy, history (the reformation and renaissance in particular), humanism, theology, and other important aspects of our human background and endeavors would find voids in this book. But this book has been written primarily for those who live and work on the concrete, action side of our society and not for those of us who live in the abstract, conceptual realm of ideas. To flood the work with more details would diminish its usefulness in its intended sphere. A few "big trees" have been examined in the "forest of reality." The author believes the ethical "forest" has been generally and fairly represented.

The question we are culturally impaled upon is, "How do we *determine* and *validate* what is right and wrong?" For centuries our culture overwhelmingly accepted the Judaic/Christian presupposition that God had acted and spoken in history (the Biblical record) and that he had provided the answer to what was "good and right" and "bad and wrong." This assumption, while still held by many individuals, has been rigorously challenged. In great numbers, others have modified their view about the record of God's having provided such help, while still others have rejected such a thesis altogether. The cultural consensus has, in any case, been destroyed.

In Chapters 2-6 we examine our culture's conflicting ethics and how the dominant groups in our society struggle with the disjoining question, "How do we *determine* and *validate* what is right and wrong?" This discussion enhances the readers' understanding of both their own ethical stance and what "camp" they stand in with regard to this central question. Our answer to the question has profound implications. It determines the ethical routes and directions we travel. Many people trying to resolve a practical problem—do we adopt a policy of "nondiscrimination" or one of "affirmative action," as an example—pass each other like trains in the night because they have very different ethical assumptions. Learning to practically identify peoples' ethical persuasions and how these give direction to their actions (Chapter 7) as well as learning to defend or justify our own position (Chapter 8) are absolutely necessary if we are to understand one another and formulate a strategy in the hope of achieving reconciliation. Clear, concrete illustrations are given on "how" both of these are undertaken and done.

Then the *consequential* aspects associated with subscribing to one of the dominant ethical systems is exposed, as a major segment of each ethic is applied in answering the question, "What are our corporations' social responsibilities?" The question is answered in Chapter 9 by structuring a five-step procedure through the formulation of the necessary presuppositional questions that will expose and identify the disjoining ethical choices that *must be made* in answering this most perplexing question. Once the principles and procedures are understood, they may be applied to any social responsibility question or problem. This does not imply, however, that there will be a broad cultural consensus on one's solution. There will *not* be one because the choices made at the various ethical junctures—they are clearly identified—will differ, resulting in different proposed solutions. Our ethical schizophrenia will continue to pervade our culture so long as we have divergent views on how we are to determine and validate what is right and wrong.

Because ethical schizophrenia is not going to be resolved in the near future, the book ends (Chapter 10) by developing fourteen concrete and practical suggestions for elevating the level of ethical conduct. These can be subscribed to by almost all people, independent of their particular ethical system. They will aid everyone ethically since it is the premise of this book that "good" is better than "bad" and "right" is to be preferred over "wrong."

ACKNOWLEDGEMENTS

The person most directly responsible for my development as an integrator of thoughts from an interdisciplinary perspective is Dr. Francis A. Schaeffer. This gentlemen and scholar does not know me, but I know and have been deeply influenced by his writings. As early as 1969, his work proved extremely helpful to me in pulling together many loose ends of my own thinking. In some important ways, he is my intellectual mentor.

Another person who has been extremely important to this book is Mary Anne Wilbourne, my secretary. But that inadequately describes her. A dyslexic—the author is one—may be a tenacious plugger, but he can always use lots of help. This book has been through seven drafts and reflects the answering by her of many hundreds of questions on sentence structure, style, spelling, punctuation, and other niceties of the English language. All of this help has been offered, upon request, with a pleasant smile, great patience, and a spirit of encouragement that has made me feel creative, competent, and significant. That is tact and grace at its best.

And how many men or women are able to begin a book with a publisher's contract for it in their hands before a single sentence of the material has even been penned? For those of you that have never written a book, this is not the norm. It was the fact, however, in this case, and it does two things for an author. It makes him work all the harder because of the confidence expressed in him and it removes tremendous pressure by knowing that the finished product will be accepted. Bob Dame gave me such freedom and it is deeply appreciated.

Few writers like the details associated with footnotes and the bibliography. This author is no exception. All of this tedious work was put into its proper form by a very diligent and proficient student assistant, Miss Lisa C. Martin, an English major at the University of Richmond. Many thanks to her.

I am also very grateful to have an administrative head like Dean Thomas L. Reuschling. His support was shown in a number of ways, but especially in arranging for me to take a sabbatical leave to do post-doctoral study at the University of St. Andrews in Scotland, which proved to be immensely helpful in preparing this book. Some key elements of my thinking were sharpened, matured, and integrated during that time of study and reflection. His encouragement and support have been generously given and are much appreciated.

RCC

CONTENTS

Contents xi

EVERYBODY IS AN ETHICIST—
JUST LISTEN TO THEM

Ethical "back-seat drivers" are everywhere and they will second guess any and every decision a manager makes. They appear at stockholders meetings, introduce themselves through the mail, and come disguised as journalists and reporters. They come from every walk of life. These ethical eagle-eyes question relocation decisions, complain about "their" corporation being engaged in defense contract work or announce that some particular form of discrimination is being practiced. And what is particularly embarrassing to corporations is that, on occasion, their protagonists appear to the watching world to be right. And when they think they are right, they will seek injunctions or threaten to organize a boycott. One thing is certain. We are living in a time of ethical turmoil—everyone seems willing to challenge anyone.

How does a manager cope with all this ethical second guessing? First, one must learn to recognize and come to understand the major ethical positions in whatever culture we operate in. Then managers must grasp the significance of the fact that their decisions make them *de facto* "professors of moral philosophy." That is, their impact-laden decisions and actions automatically embody a set of ethical values which may come into conflict with those held by many other people. Thus, a reaction, which can vary from an unexpressed difference of opinion to the formation of an international boycott, is almost certain to be present. In this chapter, the need for every manager to accept and take seriously his or her role as an automatic maker of *affectual* value judgments is stressed. Every value judgment sits atop a host of unstated ethical assumptions. These hidden assumptions not only underlie our basic decisions but also our acts of implementation. If a decision is to withstand a challenge, any presuppositions or "hidden agenda" must also be identified and incorporated as a part of management's process of justification. Managers must have the courage to openly state and discuss the bases for a decision. If they cannot or do not, a good ethical position can be made to appear immoral or indefensible.

Decision makers need to realize they are operating in an ethically schizophrenic society, one having the inability to develop an ethical consensus. We have a newer value system flooding in on top of an old ethic. The result is an ethical riptide. Chapters 2 and 3 lay out for examination the genesis and formation of the competing value systems and identify the foundational assumptions upon which they both rest. Understanding the competing values and their underlying assumptions is essential if specific decisions are to be successfully defended in the face of well articulated challenges.

Chapters 4, 5, and 6 look at the very subtle and most influential cause of change in our culture's ethical outlook. Changing a culture's ethic is as dramatic a phenomenon as the performing of a brain transplant would be for a human. It might be questioned if the individual should even be called the same person following the operation. And so it is with our culture. But what has given birth to the ethical upheaval we are experiencing? The change is produced by having an entirely new *process* employed when answering the questions, "How do we know truth?" The new process generates a radically different answer. Our concept of "truth" (what is in agreement with reality) is the foundation of all our value systems and judgments. Today our culture determines moral truth very differently from the way it did one hundred or even fifty years ago. This is seen in the fact that formerly ethical truth was thought to be fixed (absolute truth) while today it is conceived of by many people as being tentative (relative or situational truth). This change profoundly affects one's view of the world and how we treat one another.

When environmentalists tell the corporation it ought to put the water back in the river just as clean as it took the water out, and corporate management calls for a cost/benefit analysis, we are observing the unfolding of an ethical conflict. And the first thing needed, if reconciliation between the parties is to be effective, is an understanding and appreciation of the "ethical highways" the two groups are traveling on. It goes without saying that if you want to drive from Atlanta to Chicago, you do not take the interstate highway to Los Angeles. The ethical routes of debate are as simple and definable as highway routes. When people are on different highways, how can they agree on the destination? Disagreements should be expected in these cases. If understanding and reconciliation are to occur, there must be mutually respected and agreed upon ethical destinations. Chapter 7 sets the ethical highways out so that any decision maker can tell where the people they are conversing with are coming from and where they are going.

The most difficult part of any ethical discussion, however, is justifying the specific position taken. This is because people feel intellectually naked when called upon to reveal the most basic value foundations that underlie their actions. Decisions rest on value judgments. As an illustration, who wants to admit publicly that their judgment rests on intuitive feelings that are embedded in the way they interpret "the natural order of things" (only one of a number of possible justifying bases for a position)? Consequently, people often respond defensively by saying, "That is just the way it is!" or, "That is the way it has always been." Thus there is no real communication, justification, or understanding. Chapter 8 examines some of the most common systems of justification and encourages their use.

Next, in Chapter 9 all of the material is brought together and focused on the issues of human dignity, equality and/or inequality, and distributive justice as a means of formulating a set of underlying principles with which one can deal with the many problems associated with the broad field of corporate social responsibility. The intent is to both establish the need for and ability of the reader to develop a few general principles that can be used by him or her as the broad array of different problems are encountered in the social responsibility arena. Since we are frequently being presented with newly perceived problems, we need some principles to help us. The individuals with a well defined set of ethical principles are in a better position to both articulate and affect responsible solutions to such problems.

And the book closes (Chapter 10) with fourteen practical steps that can be followed by anyone who wishes to be more sensitive and careful with regard to the ethical aspects that are a part of all decision making. These common sense guides are ethical "elevators" that are intended to encourage and support good ethical practices both at the level of "what" is done and in the "how" it is done. More of our ethical temperament is revealed in the *carrying out* of a decision than it is in the *making* of a basic decision. *Wanting to be* ethical is the first necessary step to being ethical and these "guides" are helps to that end.

Figure 1.1 outlines, in the broadest categories, the basic world groups that wrestle with the question, "What is right?" It must be added that these groups are by no means homogeneous within their own ranks. As an example, atheists may be for and against abortion or Christians may be "hawks" or "doves." These twelve groups do, however, have defined *grounds* for their beliefs about what is right and wrong. The "grounds" are represented on the outer perimeter of the chart. Some "grounds" are of a "natural order" and others are of a "divine order." They, too, differ in perspective from group to group and even within groups.

This book makes no attempt to deal with each of these groups, since that would be counterproductive for our purposes. Only the philosophical humanists, theological humanists, neo-orthodox Christians, and orthodox Christians are examined in any depth. (The Jewish perspective is included but in less detail.) These groups were chosen because they cover the overwhelming majority of people in our culture. While there are other groups in our culture who have some significant influence, the benefit to be gained by including them was considered marginal; therefore they were excluded.

DECISION MAKERS ARE PHILOSOPHERS   All ethical considerations revolve around how we ought to "be" and "act" as humans. And since managers take action, they are deeply involved in ethics all the time, whether they are conscious of it or not. Many tend to think of ethics as a dry subject belonging to professional philosophers who spend their time splitting verbal hairs. But ethics permeates all human life and activity. Ethical thought and behavior are as automatic and involuntary as the beating of a heart, although not as regulated. We are normally as unconscious of this as we are of all our involuntary functions.

Figure 1.1

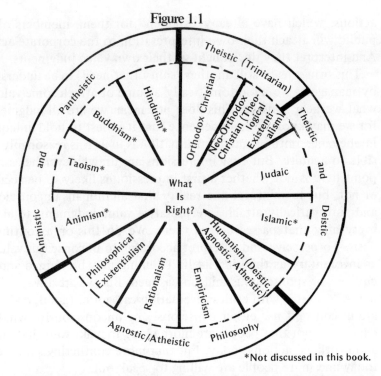

*Not discussed in this book.

The big difference is that the involuntary character of being involved with ethics can be brought to the conscious level of the mind and interacted with internally. We can change and grow ethically. Ethical thinking is part of the automatic thought process which accompanies all behavior.

The formal study of ethics is the contemplation of what is "good" and "right" in matters of human intentions, motives, traits, and actions along with their consequences and results. Our human activity simply mirrors our intentions, motives, traits and actions, which produce a myriad of qualitative and quantitative results. We live out an assumed, conscious, implied or explicit ethic, whether or not we ever formally study the subject. How we live exposes our ethics and makes us subject to being read, almost like a book.

Most of us have heard, "Your actions speak so loud I cannot hear a word you are saying." Actions and words are both important, but should a conflict appear between them, actions will be interpreted as the real message. Actions are the louder message, reflecting a philosophy. Business men, by their actions, are exposing a philosophy. In this day and age, if managers refuse to explain their actions, which have already "spoken" for them, members of the public will attach their own interpretation to the corporate action. And interpret they do, in light of their own value judgments.

This brings us to still another reality that needs to be understood by managers. We all automatically assume or attach some value to what we hear and see. This does not mean we are all judgmental, for we may know from experience that it is best to hold judgments in abeyance until as much information is in as it is reasonably possible to acquire. But first impressions are drawn nevertheless. The point here is not whether a first impression is likely to be accurate or not, but to reinforce the reality that all humans unconsciously and automatically attach interpretative value judgments to almost everything that passes before them. We do this on a continuous basis. To perceive and interpret according to unconscious values is as involuntary as thinking itself. Thinking may be trained and disciplined or spontaneous and unreasoned. But we are always thinking. And so it is with ethics. Evaluation categories (good, bad, etc.) are in constant use either consciously or unconsciously. What has changed is not that people are more likely to make value judgments about others' actions today, but that more conflicting values exist today and more people are willing to speak out.

A concrete illustration will help sharpen the assertion that we all automatically and involuntarily attach values to what we think, do, see, and hear. Imagine that Tom Successful, sales manager for a national industrial products company is just entering a conference room where sixteen sales people from Region Three are awaiting him.

> "Good morning, ladies and gentlemen," he intones in a cheerful, ringing voice. "Every last one of you is to be commended for your performance this past month. You have really done a super job. Nationwide, sales in our industry are off 30% from this time last year and we have only experienced a 5% decline in physical volume. Dollarwise we are actually 4% higher than a year ago. That is super and you should all have a great sense of accomplishment.

Before we eavesdrop on the thoughts of several of the sales people, who just heard this introductory comment, we ought to stop and identify just a few of the value (ethical) judgments made by our imaginary sales manager. He judged that the entire group had done a good job in the past month. He did not mention that at the previous month's meeting the goal had been set 2% higher than was actually achieved. He had decided to leave the negative aspect out and only report the positive data, which, in his opinion, did reflect a wonderful accomplishment. Even his data selection and method of presentation both reflect ethical judgments. He even went so far as to make a judgment about how they should feel concerning their accomplishments. His whole opening statement is loaded with ethical qualities.

Those who attend such meetings automatically react to all they hear and attach value-laden interpretations to every aspect of what *has* and *has not* transpired. How might sales people react to the introductory statement ascribed to Tom Successful? Jim Broadgauge might think, "Well, Tom took the realities pretty well. Our telling him and letting him know last month that most of us thought he was pushing a little hard seems to have paid some dividends. I hope he doesn't screw the vise too tight this morning for the coming month. Things are tough out there." Barbara Hidden could conclude, "The phoney! More nice words to grease us up to get us to run even harder this month. What a hypocrite!" And Bob Reflective may reason, "I guess Tom is right; we have done a pretty good job given the conditions. Yeah, that's great. I always feel guilty that I haven't done better. Tom seems to always know when I need some encouragement or a gentle push."

The three sales people all heard the same words, but the values they attached to the message as a result of their personal interpretations are fundamentally different while retaining one common element. The common element is "I always ascribe *values* to what goes on around me." The values they impute, however, really reveal more about themselves than they do about Tom Successful, the sales manager.

Jim Broadgauge perceived some "good" things—Tom listened, heard, reacted well, and has reduced the pressure. He hopes this "good" continues. Jim has focused on, and attached value to, the process/performance aspects of his boss. Barbara Hidden perceives some "bad" things—Tom is an actor (hypocrite), manipulator, and a user of people. She impugns her boss's intention and motives. And Bob Reflective has interpreted almost everything in terms of his personal feelings and needs. He "feels good" as a result of what has been said and attached "good" values to his boss.

One message was delivered to different interpreters who each ascribe different *values* to the person, process, and consequences. This illustration does not even scratch the surface of the complexity of our automatic and involuntary process of making value judgments concerning all that goes on around us. Should executives be surprised then, when others question almost every decision they make?

All of us who make decisions need to understand ourselves as active philosophers, whether or not we would be formally classified as a "philosopher." What we need to be consciously aware of is that all of our thinking and behavior are value-laden. When the majority of those associated with an event have the same values, few questions are raised on the value plane. But when values which differ are brought into relationship with each other, differences and conflicts are soon apparent. Most of these conflicts reflect fundamental differences in our perceptions about "right" and "wrong" or testify to differences in "how" objectives should be pursued. But in our culture today, differences are many and real. We must learn how to cope with them constructively.

ETHICAL   Ethical presuppositions are value-laden
ASSUMPTIONS   assumptions lying beneath the subject
                          under consideration that are believed to
be factual or logical and which are necessary for, or contingently related to, the matter being examined. All of our thoughts and actions in life rest on top of a myriad of such assumptions. These assumptions are the "feet" of all our decisions. They carry the decision along. And they are most often taken for granted just like our real feet are until they are stepped on or hurt in some other manner.

When presuppositions are described as our decision "feet," it is another way of saying that most decisions to do something in life flow rather automatically from assumed truths and concepts of appropriateness which have been learned and routinized. These assumptions are taken for granted and are rarely pondered. That someone else would think and act differently is hardly contemplated.

For example, assume two men go into a fashionable restaurant and order identical meals. The meals are served and immediately the two gentlemen reveal very different behavior patterns, exhibiting unstated and probably even unconscious presuppositions. The first man takes up the salt shaker and showers his meat, potatoes, and vegetables rather liberally before he has tasted anything. His conduct is a habit borne along by the assumption that the food will need to be seasoned. The second gentlemen tastes each portion ordered and only seasons his potatoes with a light sprinkling of salt. He began his meal with the assumption that it might arrive having already been properly seasoned. Their presuppositions were the controlling influence on their concrete actions. Assumptions are generally the guiding factor in decisions.

The overwhelming majority of our actions in life are just that automatic and are borne along on harmless assumptions which are usually learned from those who were our role models. We eat, dress, drive, and do hundreds of things on this basis. But as our personal assumptions begin to impact others, we need to become more conscious of our presuppositions and the role they play. If the first gentlemen in the above example had reached across the table and salted his associate's meal, we could imagine a host of possible reactions ranging from silent consternation to a full blown confrontation. Should we expect a smaller range of attitudes to be manifested between proponents and opponents of the nuclear generation of electricity with its accompanying questions on matters of operating safety and waste disposal? These positions, too, rest on a long list of presuppositions.

Every decision in business rests on a number of assumptions. Whether management is trying to decide on how "required" or how "voluntary" executive participation in the local community fund drive should be, or how to deal with an ineffective fifty-five year old plant manager with thirty years of service (fire, retire early, transfer, demote, or support), each and every consideration rests on assumptions about priorities, responsibilities, conflicts, the future, and other similar concerns. Most of our ethical debate on such issues flows from challenges raised about our assumptions. In our culture there is less and less consensus on what is appropriate on every ethical front.

Managers need to develop and cultivate their ability to recognize, articulate, and defend their presuppositions. But what does one do when his assumptions are challenged? Most business decision makers try to quantify their variables so as to be able to express themselves in terms of possibilities and probabilities. They feel more comfortable in this framework than any other. Sooner or later, however, decision makers learn that quantifiable probabilities expressed in terms of efficiency, productivity, and profitability do not necessarily coincide with ethical decisions. How much chemical is harmful, how much risk is acceptable, and other such questions are not resolved by quantifiable data alone but await a value judgment. When an executive makes a decision, he or she must be prepared to justify the decision.

HOW TO   Almost everyone responsible for making
JUSTIFY   decisions feels defensive and uncomfort-
                                able when called upon to justify a specific
action. Why? Because a whole new set of presuppositions related
to our perception and use of authority, responsibility, and accountability are implicitly called into question. Many individuals
react defensively to their challengers, as if they were "out of order,"
"have no business asking such questions," or are "self-appointed
do-gooders who do more harm than good."

Reactions such as these are hindrances to offering a sound justification. Vindicating a decision needs to be an offensive act and
not a defensive one. To use a sports analogy, when the ball is in
your court, you are in a position to go on the offensive. It almost
never helps the case to challenge another's *right to ask* for a justification of an action. This is generally taken to imply that the re-
spondent does not have a good answer. Managers often do not offer
a good response, not because their actions are not sustainable, but
because those responsible do not understand their presuppositions
or how to justify them.

A response which reflects an attitude that "the corporation has
a *right* to take this action" is not a justification. A "right" is a
claim, but does not in itself warrant your having made the particular decision. And statements to the effect that "this is the way it
has always been done" will not do either. Or, worse yet, attitudes
reflecting belligerence such as "that is just the way it is" prove in-
flammatory and do damage. All of these examples have their genesis in an assumed authority base. Claiming authority does not even
address the issue of the appropriateness of a particular action. The
questioner may well concede that the decision makers have the
authority, but are, in fact, challenging its responsible use. This is
most often the central issue.

Leaders need to realize that doing a responsible job and being
proficient in defending the action does not guarantee greater acceptance or necessarily reduce the number of challenges. While the
ultimate correctness of a decision is only realized over time, it is
the accuracy of the presuppositions and justification system that
serves as the foundation upon which the decision is carried out.
The justification represents the depths to which one can go in
expressing why something should or should not be done. It is the
"bottom of the well." It is the bedrock.

What are these foundations? There are a fairly large number of possible bases of defense, but in this book, we will limit our consideration to one negative and three positive categories of justification. Their in-depth exploration is undertaken in Chapter 8, but they need to be introduced here. The "rightness" or "wrongness" of a position may be justified by appealing to the natural order, a metaphysical base, intuitive and "feeling" knowledge, or by denying and limiting the possibilities of justification.

Appealing to the natural order or "nature of things" is a naturalist position. To illustrate, a business might have a policy forbidding their purchasing agents from accepting any gifts from their suppliers. The firm might justify this by stating that people's innate make-up subjects them to the possibility of being tempted, which could become so great as to influence or impair their otherwise sound judgment. Since it is not possible to predetermine when the phenomenon of temptation will occur, the policy has been established which removes any possibility of its influence.

The stated policy and accompanying justification do not remove or inhibit a complaint that the policy is too restrictive or that we have even misread the nature of things. Someone could argue that simply requiring the agents to routinely list for their boss all gifts received along with the donor's name and company he represents would be sufficient to curtail undue influence. It is evident that debate is not hard to generate.

There are also a number of metaphysical bases of justification. These appeal to a "belief" about a deity or a set of invisible principles assumed to undergird the observable. This is often the explanation of "why" the nature of things should be interpreted in a particular way. This is one step deeper than merely appealing to natural observation. Our culture rested for centuries on a host of Judaic/Christian presuppositions. These were acceptable because the majority of the populace believed them. As an illustration, business, labor, government, and the general public accepted until post World War II various Blue Laws or Sunday Closing Laws. This reflected the historical acceptance of the Biblical command to "Remember the Sabbath day, to keep it holy" (Exodus 20:8). The metaphysical justification was the belief that God had given this commandment for the good of His people.

The next area of justification is expanding and is particularly difficult for businesses to cope with, because it does not lend itself to an objective form of scrutiny. This is justification based on intuition and feelings. Intuition is a form of instant knowledge. It is not held because of the nature of things observed, but is held because the person has been in the presence of, and been related to, an object, a person, or a situation. As an illustration, "I just know that if we let the Big Trouble Corporation build on the Peaceful Pasture property that our whole county is in for bad times. Mark my word, big corporations are accompanied by nothing but trouble. Our county supervisors may be speaking to us about economic glory but it will only end in a mess." Or, you will hear one manager say to another one, "Yes, I spent the whole morning with Henry (potential candidate for a position in the firm) and I just do not believe he is the man for us. I don't know if I could trust him." (There is nothing in Henry's background to imply that he is not trustworthy.) You can challenge such "knowledge" but it does not yield to demonstrable logic.

Finally, there are the limiting and denying forms of justification that must be understood and contended with. There are plenty of people who will dare anyone to justify their position. They insist that all values must be understood as a personal view, a relative view, a possible view, or be classified as a non-normative view. This is the most rapidly growing group involving themselves in ethical debate. Both their power and Achilles heel are found in their demand for "proof" and the presuppositions which are attached to it. Chapters 4, 5, and 6 specifically address the nature of proof associated with ethical questions, so this concern will be delayed until then.

The subtle force of the limiting and denial groups is found in their undermining the belief that it is possible to establish an ethical consensus grounded on reason. If an ethical reality which is based on reason is beyond our grasp, then we are either left with ethical anarchy or having ethical "fallout"—a concern for ethics when there is no true basis for ethics at all—which would be an unintended by-product resulting from the decision-making process. One of our culturally unresolved questions is whether we are moving to a new consensus, toward ethical anarchy, ethical totalitarianism, or an ill-defined ethical position where the possibility of ethics is denied.

The force of this ethical confusion is discovered in the many publicly exposed cases of poor ethics where someone consciously and purposefully acted in a manner he or she believed to be ethically "wrong" but "best" for themselves or the corporation. When people develop conceptual thought patterns that become fraught with conflict between what is believed *right* and what is presumed *best,* we are indeed in ethical pain. Our culture is exhibiting a lot of ethical pain.

Given all of this, is it any wonder that business ethics is so often considered an impenetrable swamp filled with irreconcilable conflicts where there is no real hope of building a genuine consensus? This is discouraging and causes many to wonder if there is anything to be gained in trying. When people are hurting deeply and their self respect and basic dignity are under attack, there is all the more reason to re-examine what is truly valuable.

COPING WITH VALUE CONFLICTS How are we to cope with all the value conflicts that surround us? It is no easy task. Keeping our ethical feet under us is like climbing out of a river after wading for smallmouth bass and attempting to climb a steep mud bank after a rainstorm, with a string of fish in one hand and our fishing tackle in the other. What are our chances of getting to the top without falling? If we take no regard for the situation and simply charge up the slope, we are almost guaranteed to fall. But examining the slippery bank for an exposed root here and a small outcropping of rock there will probably afford us an opportunity to successfully maneuver the hazard. We need to be as careful with our ethical feet.

In all truth, the real problem confronting all of us is not so much knowing what is righ and ethical as it is having the resolve to do what is ethically correct. The trouble arises within ourselves when we are confronted with the choice between what is believed to be ideally right and what appears as an immediate opportunity to gain a desired or even necessary end by a means not completely in conformity with our ethical standards. By this we are subtly drawn into a process of rationalization and compromise all too familiar to every human being. This is how so many gradually slip into the practice of ethical pragmatism where "right" is subordinated to "best," and "purity" is subordinated to "practicality." This is our culture's dominant ethical temptation and all too frequent practice. The "end" is used to justify the "means." We know better—metaphysically, naturally, or intuitively!

Another very real problem is making choices in light of culturally accepted practices when our personal desire would be that a totally different or higher standard be followed rather than the prevailing one. Can we risk appearing like a salmon always swimming upstream against the flow? Once again the rationalization process comes to the fore. After enough people rationalize compromises for a long enough period of time, a lower level of ethical conduct becomes the cultural norm. The cliche, "When in Rome do as the Romans do" is offered as a solution all too often when one asks for an opinion while sharing personal reservations about a particular decision. The advice, while surely well intended, only masks the conscionable concern and does nothing to answer the deeper questions. Well meaning friends and business associates so often seem to pull one another toward the easy short-run decision that promises an immediate reward.

There is the additional problem of finding ourselves in a situation where we are unaware of the ethical ramifications or are so untrained as to be merely culturally responsive. The decision makers pick up their ethics by cultural osmosis and respond later as well trained "cultural bird dogs." They point to historic values and then are dumbfounded, hurt, and eventually angry when they are criticized or challenged for having done so. And then confusion slowly engulfs us like the fog rolling ashore from sea. The old is swallowed and the new emerges.

And to be sure, there are the uncaring—the ethical dandelions that are blown about by every wind and land wherever it is convenient. They are not interested in ethics and only find it a bother. They are a minority and generally do not function well in groups or teams. They do not set the tone, but do add to the confusion.

Another group of minorities, who generations ago were the shapers of our culture, are the ethical idealists. They drew their ideals from the Reformational and Renaissance standard-bearers. For reasons of religious and philosophical conviction, they were uncompromising and inflexible. They held a set of standards and were willing to defend them with their lives. Today these types are seen as narrow, idealistic, impractical, fanatic, or categorized by other uncomplimentary terms. But for them, what was considered "right" stood high on their priority list. In Chapter 2, we will examine their influence and current whereabouts.

Realizing all of this still does not help us make a choice or cope with the conflicting values that are ever present and demand our attention. For this we need to turn to the basic issue of accountability. To whom am I accountable? The answer is again rooted in the systems of justification mentioned previously (see Chapter 8). If we justify our decisions on a metaphysical plane we look to a personal or nonpersonal deity and the naturally revealed standards of righteousness. We are presumed to be accountable to the deity or within a process established by the deity. If, on the other hand, we look to the natural order of things, another human, or ourselves for justification, then we must look to other people or within ourselves for our standard of conduct. Here we assume we are accountable either to another human or to ourselves. These are our choices. We are accountable either to a deity, another human, or ourselves.

On a grander scale, cultures tend to be stable when there is a high degree of ethical consensus within them at the presuppositional level. When assumptions march together, there is solidarity and strength. Conversely, no culture can remain strong and viable indefinitely if the ethical consensus is destroyed. We are living in a time when the old consensus is being challenged by many and dismantled and replaced by others. Will the old be revived; will its replacement be a new consensus; or will a group of unreconciled and competing value judgments rule us? The resolution is not totally clear but the war between, and even within, the ethics is abundantly clear. In Chapter 2, there is an examination of this struggle.

BIBLIOGRAPHY

Allport, Gordon; Philip Vernon; and Gardner Lindzey, *Study of Values.* Boston, Mass.: Houghton Mufflin, 1931.

Cavanaugh, Gerald F., *American Business Values in Transition.* New Jersey: Prentice-Hall, Inc., 1976.

Hofstadter, Richard, *Social Darwinism in American Thought.* New York: Braziller, 1959.

Likert, Renis, *The Human Organization: Its Management and Value.* New York: McGraw-Hill, 1967.

Nef, John U., *Cultural Foundations of Industrial Civilization.* Cambridge, England: Cambridge University Press, 1958.

Nosow, Sigmund and William H. Form, *Man, Work, and Society.* New York: Basic Books, 1962.

Rokeach, Milton, *Study of Values.* New York: Free Press, 1973.

Schlesinger, Arthur M., *Paths of American Thought,* ed. Arthur M. Schlesinger, Jr. and Morton White. Boston, Mass.: Houghton Mifflin, 1963.

Schumpeter, Joseph A., *Capitalism, Socialism, and Democracy.* London: Allen and Unwin, 1943.

Sutton, Francis X.; Seymour E. Harris; Carl Kaysen; and James Tobin; *The American Business Creed.* Cambridge, Mass.: Harvard University Press, 1956.

TWO

THE OLD VALUES

AN ETHICAL
EARTHQUAKE

Our culture's ethical conflict has already been likened to a riptide where two layers of water are moving over and under one another in such a way as to make human maneuver hazardous. A geological fault line, such as the San Andreas fault on the west coast, provides an even clearer analogy of what is going on ethically. Changing characteristics within the earth's core, deep below the visible surface, create pressures which cause the great surface plates to collide, rub, and shatter against one another. The tremors created by this collision and friction can, and on occasion have caused, devastating damage.

When changes take place in what people perceive to be right and wrong, these shifts will manifest themselves in the form of changed behavior or the raising of new questions which may run counter to their old values and beliefs. Actions that might have been accepted by them ten years ago are now denounced. Harmony can be turned into disharmony. Trust may be replaced by distrust. The old is challenged by the new. People become divided on more and more issues.

Ethically our culture is experiencing such an earthquake. It is

17

caught in a riptide. Choose your own analogy but cultural tremors are its side effects. Some argue we are in a time of decay. Others believe it is a time of growth and adjustment that will result in a stronger and more viable condition. Our personal presuppositions shape our individual prognostications. But no one argues about whether or not we are experiencing inner conflict. We are.

Two major ethical systems that are competing with one another in our culture today are outlined in Figure 2.1. Many individuals

Figure 2.1   The Old Ethic–Reformational/Renaissance Ethic–The God/Man Ethic

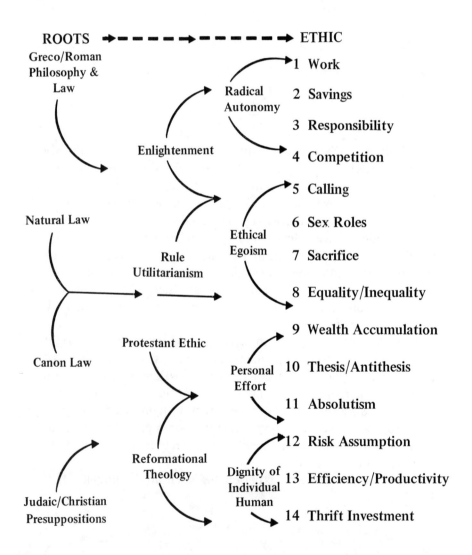

strongly identify with one of the courses while rejecting the other. Other individuals accept one of the systems as the predominant value structure for business purposes, while finding the other more appealing at the personal level. But most people are trying to merge and synthesize the two. Like most of us who have never learned to mix oil and water so as to achieve one homogeneous liquid, the majority of decision makers are ill-equipped to handle this kind of ethical conflict. This leads them to either choose an ethical course

Figure 2.1 (Continued) The New Ethic–Empiricist/Rationalist/Existentialist Ethic–The Man Ethic

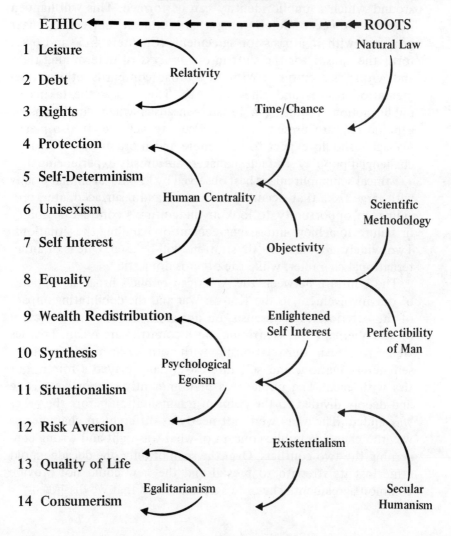

and defend it; make an effort to compartmentalize their life into "my business world" and "my private life" in an attempt to justify their behavioral differences; or accept a life of conflict with its accompanying guilt, while resignedly allowing that "this is just the way things are." Culturally, these alternatives are creating a form of ethical schizophrenia.

What is ethical schizophrenia? First, the phrase is used to connote a cultural condition and not the state of an individual. Second, the phrase is not used to imply a problem within one or the other of the competing ethics. The condition exists where there is no ethical consensus in the culture about what is right or wrong and around which a public identity can be formed. This will happen when the *process* of determining what is ethically correct no longer produces with it a basis for agreement. (Chapters 4, 5, and 6 set forth the causes for the shift in our *process* of determining right and wrong as a culture.) Without a broad consensus, ethical fragmentation results and rules the day. This makes the taking of public action, requiring a broad consensus when conditions of genuine risk are present, very difficult to achieve. It also means managers should expect to have more and more of their decisions challenged publicly. In fact, managers are already experiencing this.

Ethical schizophrenia is best observed by looking at similar events with large risks that occurred in the past and resurfaced later, providing an opportunity to look at the culture's contrasting ability or failure to achieve internal agreement on handling the situations. Two widely documented illustrations will be used. One is of an international character, while the other is domestic.

The contrast between the American public's broad acceptance of our involvement in the Korean War and the debilitating impact of the deteriorating consensus on our ability to successfully carry on the Vietnam War is striking. Both countries are Asian. Treaties were involved in our relationship with both. Concepts of freedom, self determination, and self interest initially played a role in our ties with each. The public was predominantly supportive of one and deeply divided to the point of fragmentation before the other was ended. The wars were not nearly as different in character as was the changing public concept of what was right and wrong concerning the two conflicts. Over the span of only one decade an old ethic lost its strength to prevail and the new could not provide common agreement. The only agreement was that we disagreed.

The shift in beliefs concerning the role of women in society is another example reflecting our cultural change. No longer do men agree with men, women agree with women, or men with women on the appropriate roles of men and women. There was a broad consensus on this question fifty years ago. Today there is not.

The list of issues, where consensus prevailed for many generations and now does not, is growing rapidly. These changes are not mere realignments within old groups or a newly emerging revitalized pluralism where individuals and groups align themselves for specific ends. This is ethical schizophrenia—a growing inability to reach an ethical consensus and a more fundamental emerging doubt about the possibility of achieving general agreement on important issues. Pluralism was born out of different special and competing interests which all rested atop reasonably homogeneous ethical presuppositions. Ethical schizophrenia emerges from conflict within and between ethical assumptions producing doubts about our ability to even know what is right or wrong.

More people in our culture are being equipped intellectually to state their objections to another's actions, ideas, and values than are being prepared to offer constructive, positive substitutes for the positions being attacked. This reflects a widespread doubt about our ability to empirically, rationally, existentially, or religiously determine right from wrong any longer. The psychology of "fault finding" is smothering the belief that people can substantiate an ethic. Ethical earthquakes abound in such a situation.

RISE OF THE OLD VALUES   The old values have their roots in antiquity. Today, however, these values are being surrounded like the posts of a pier on a coastal mudflat when the tide comes in. Are the old value posts solid and will the ethical pier stand, only to see the new tide once again go out and leave the old intact? Or, are the value posts so worm eaten that the rising tide will finally carry the old pier away, leaving only the stobs in the mud as a reminder of days gone by?

Take a moment and examine Figure 2.1 in some detail. Then imagine that all the cultural institutions (family, business, government, religion, education, social, etc.) are located in the seam of the book between the two pages. The left page represents the old ethical force moving from left to right and the right page embodies the new force moving from right to left. Our culture is under pressure in the middle. The forces are subtle and pervasive like the pull of gravity causing a great tidal movement. Only occasionally do they clash in great force as in a court case or on the picket line, but the real battle is for the minds of the populace.

As we move from the outside edge of Figure 2.1 toward the middle seam, we cover a span of time that moves from the seedbed of the ethic, through its growth, to its demonstrable fruit. The fourteen items facing each other across the seam are the major ingredients or components of the individual ethic. The ingredients are ideas or thoughts that have "rightness" or "wrongness" associated with them in the mind of the decision maker.

We will turn first to the old ethic and look at its genesis, growth, and particular ideals. Volumes have been written on each and every individual part of it, but an overview is essential if our true cultural conflict and ethical confusion are to be understood. Like a piece of hemp rope which is comprised of thousands of individual strands of fiber, historic phenomena reflect the interaction and reverberating influences of countless events. Only a bare skeletal outline of those things contributing to this ethic will be given in this work.

Between 1350 and 1650 A.D., two giant forces swept across Europe and the surrounding regions. These movements were spontaneous. They were physical, intellectual, and spiritual in character and influence. They rubbed each other; they mixed and intermixed with each other; they fought each other; they loved each other; they went their separate ways; and they lived intimately with each other. They were married. They are commonly known as the Reformation and the Renaissance. These two great shapers of the human mind flowed onto the scene simultaneously and provided the vast majority of the stimulation and motivation that undergirded the development of modern western civilization. For this reason, the resulting ethic that emerged is called, in this book the Reformational/Renaissance Ethic (R/R Ethic). This old ethic was a God/Man Ethic. It had deep roots in a concept of God and embraced an idea about free, creative men. We will begin our very brief historic journey by first taking a quick look at the contribution of the renaissance to the R/R Ethic.

FORCES OF THE RENAISSANCE   The very word "renaissance" has the power to bring to mind many different connotations. Some would think of the great artisans such as Leonardo da Vinci (1452-1519), the famous

Florentine painter, engineer, architect, and sculptor; or, Michelangelo Buonarroti (1475-1564), the Italian sculptor, painter, and architect. Others might think of the political or papal history of the period. But above all, it was the rebirth of the humanistic influences that had been embodied in the classical expressions of the Greco/Roman period. Human expression and human inquiry were stirred. The bed covers that had been pulled up over the western mind with the decay of Rome were once again pulled back and the reawakening began.

The focus, however, is not to repaint a picture of the renaissance, but to pick up on and ride a few major ideas that are widely recognized as basic and fundamental to the development of the R/R Ethic. Our look will be limited to Central Europe and England, where the threads of law, philosophy, and science are most easily discerned.

Rule of Law   The very assumption that men are better ruled by law than by other men and that an internalized acceptance of the law, leading to self control, is the best access to the possibility of developing human potential was slow in developing. But the presence of this assumption and its weight served as a foundational building block for the R/R Ethic. The western mind embraced law as a friend and supporter. Law was seen as an avenue of protection from arbitrary and unjust conduct. A great interest was expressed in common law, enacted law, physical/natural law, and Biblical law. The latter of these will be handled later in the Reformational section, but "law" was a symbol of stability and represented a road to freedom and advancement.

The Roman Empire, in its vast expanse, developed a tremendous body of law and a system of adjudication within which to administer it. This was spread far and wide for the protection of the Roman citizenry. Following the demise of Roman control, the memory and seeds of much of its practice were left behind to await germination at a future time when the political and economic climate were right. The law and legal system which burst into flower centuries later was not an exact replica of the old Roman system, but its genesis was unmistakable.[1]

---

[1] Charles P. Sherman, *Roman Law in the Modern World,* Volume 1 History, (New York: Baker Voorkis and Co., 1937) pp. 1-10.

As an example, in the late medieval period a system of local courts came into being that were associated with the great commercial fairs of the day. These fairs were typically annual events and some of the larger ones lasted for considerable periods of time. The law they administered was unwritten and concerned itself, for the most part, with the enforcement of verbal contracts. The body of common law became known as the "Law Merchant." Complaints were heard before a body of jurors selected from the merchants themselves. The principal parties and their witnesses were heard and justice was rendered swiftly. The system worked well.[2] The rule of law was once again on the march.

And a whole body of common law grew up in England around property rights, developed over hundreds of years as manor lords interacted with those who lived on their land. These manors were vast land holdings given by the King to a favored subject who operated the area as a domain. Those who lived on the land had various social standings granted by the manor lord and disputes would inevitably arise. The developed practices became the common law which was adjudicated in established manor courts.[3] Due process continued to grow in importance. We were destined to be men under law. Examples abound of the growth and development of this trend.

The stability this affords a society is profound. We take for granted that our relationships and transactions are protected by the law and, should a breakdown occur, disputes can be settled fairly. Look once again at Figure 2.1. The right hand column has fourteen major elements that help make up the R/R Ethic. At least six of these elements are strongly motivated and stabilized by the presence and broadly accepted concept that it is right to be a people who are to live within the bounds of law. Who would want to *work* (1) enough to generate *savings* (2), which require a personal *sacrifice* (3), and run the *risk* (12) associated with making an *investment* (14), in order to *accumulate wealth* (9), if someone else could confiscate it without recourse?

Before the common law developed, many feudal barons and manor lords assumed that all the people who resided within their property boundaries, along with their possessions, rightfully be-

---

[2] E. A. J. Johnson and Herman E. Krooss, *The American Economy: Its Origins, Development, and Transformation,* (New Jersey: Prentice-Hall, Inc., 1960) p. 35.
[3] Johnson and Krooss, pp. 25-28.

longed to them. This certainly did not provide an incentive to work harder or inquire as to how a task might be performed more efficiently. But what we take for granted in twentieth century America—protection under the law—has not been an expected way of life for the majority of people for most of recorded history. The physical benefits we so richly enjoy would have been unheard of to this day, without our commitment to live under and by the law.

Robert Heilbroner, in a book entitled *The Making of Economic Society,* points out brilliantly that historically mankind has had only three different basic systems for taking care of production and distribution needs. People have sometimes used a system that rested on, and functioned according to, "Tradition," where a pattern of doing things is accepted over many generations because it has "always been, and worked that way." Others have employed a "Command" system where someone or a small group directed the events. And finally, there have been some who have enjoyed, for a brief span of history, the benefits of what we know as the "Market" system.[4] The Market system which was permeated with the R/R Ethic could not have existed without an unyielding, voluntary allegiance to a system of law. Without the base of law there could have been no freedom with stability and productivity.

THE STIR OF IDEAS   The next feature to be examined in our brief look at the renaissance panorama is the burst of ideas that seemed to explode on the scene. We are so idea-saturated in our culture today that it is hard for us to realize how really exciting ideas could be for people three and four hundred years ago. We have magazines, newspapers, radios, television, records, tapes, photographs, telephones, and means of traveling far and wide. The renaissance man had little of this except the burgeoning use of printing that Johann Gutenberg (1400-1468) made possible through the development of movable type. But books were still not common and neither was man's ability to read. On the other hand, we seem today to vicariously "experience" a war or a coup every month; reports of terrorists or natural disasters producing panic and terror are ever before us; heinous crime and human anguish are commonplace; and our economic fears and woes seem never to be far away. We

---

[4] Robert L. Heilbroner, *The Making of Economic Society,* (New Jersey: Prentice-Hall, Inc., 1975) pp. 13-20.

have a hard time getting excited about anything—except perhaps the hope of finding some peace and quiet—as we are stimulated to the limit of our endurance. For us, another idea is almost like finding another grain of sand on the beach. Who cares? For our renaissance forebears, an idea was received as parched ground welcomes the rain.

Another way of coming to grips with just how different the renaissance culture was from our own is to contemplate the fact that what we know or call the factors of production—land, labor, and capital—did not even exist then, as understood today.[5] Land and its accompanying resources obviously existed, but not as a saleable economic commodity. Kings had divided the land or feudal rivalries had established the boundaries, but land was not bought and sold. We take this for granted today, but four and five hundred years ago it was not very common.

People likewise were not free to move about and seek employment as today. Jobs were, for the most part, tightly controlled and regulated by guilds in the craft and commercial fields. And those who toiled on the land did not own it and thus could not dispose of it and move to another area. Most men "belonged" to the land or guild.

Furthermore, technology had not yet arisen to unlock the door to the formation of capital goods that played such a vital part in the transformation of the economic system. The renaissance period enjoyed a merchant system of economics which was destined to take on a form of merchant capitalism on its way to eventually becoming industrial capitalism. But land, labor, and capital only emerged in the modern sense during the three hundred years of economic evolution from 1500 to 1800.

By today's standards, the cultural landscape was barren. But what did take place is why historians, in looking back, have called the renaissance the time of rebirth. Ideas sprang forth like crocus from the ground, heralding the coming of spring. The masses were impoverished, uneducated, and ignorant. The few were wealthy. But the wealthy had the surplus to support a growing group of artists, people of letters, theologians, and philosophers. It was mainly from within this supported group that the intellectual ferment occurred that gave rise to a new yeast that would leaven the culture. An interest in general education and the broad devel-

[5] Heilbroner, pp. 61-62.

opment of the human intellect is itself a product of the Reformation/Renaissance period. During this time, ideas flourished and proved to be forceful influences.

Physical Universe/ While in many ways it is fictitious to
People Interaction separate the ideas and influences of this
period into Reformational and Renaissance categories, it is nevertheless useful to do so. Two streams of ideas from the Renaissance came soaring across England and Europe. Both were revolutionary. The first to come was a whole new set of ideas concerning the physical universe and how people should approach it. The "nature of things" was transformed in a flood of new perceptions. It was, however, the well-spring of the concepts that have eventually brought us in our day to a widely accepted new basis for determining "true truth." And it is the modern concept of "true truth" that has given birth to the contemporary challenge of the old ethic now being traced. So even in the active creation of one ethic, we discover the seeds of its demise.

Politics and The second stream of ideas was directed
Humanity toward political theory, human rights, and responsibilities. This stream was slower in its development but was the category of ideas most closely welded to the Reformational concepts. All of these formed the basis for the R/R Ethic. Never in history have philosophers and theologians been in such harmony.

The ideas of philosopher John Locke (1632-1704) will be used as illustrations of the emerging ideas that proved to be so influential in the development of the R/R Ethic. But Locke was not alone in speaking about such matters. He was simply well placed as an adviser to a British Minister of State and later to the Queen. In addition, his works were both written and well documented. He was an Oxford scholar who was trained theologically but eventually settled on a career in medicine. He soon gave up the active practice of medicine, however, to become the personal physician of the Earl of Shaftesbury. He resided in London and became a trusted counselor on matters of state as his social contacts were amongst the British leadership.[6] His reputation as a great philosopher was a by-product of his many activities and was not by design.

[6] W. T. Jones, *A History of Western Philosophy,* (New York: Harcourt, Brace and Company, 1952) pp. 719-720.

What were John Locke's political ideas? ". . . his political theory rests on the assumption that the moral law is an 'eternal verity' that guarantees every man certain inalienable rights and imposes certain duties."[7] He saw this as the "state of nature." He also believed that "no one ought to harm another in his life, health, liberty, or possession; for men being all the workmanship of one omnipotent and infinitely wise Maker; all the servants of one sovereign Master, sent into the world by His order and about His business; they are His property. . . ."[8] (This is one illustration of the strong bonding between theology and philosophy in that day.)

Locke also spoke strongly on political equality and the need for consent of the governed before actions affecting them were undertaken. He believed in the concept of majority rule and was a strong advocate of private property rights. He believed in religious tolerance and wrote on what he considered to be the proper relationship between the state and the church. And the state should by all means be restricted by the concept of laissez-faire.[9] These Lockean ideals, also expressed by many others during this period, were essential ingredients of the R/R Ethic. The idea of being ruled by law provided stability but the beliefs in the preservation of life, health, liberty, and private property within a laissez-faire state spoke to a newly expressed concept of the dignity of man.

**Power of
Science**

The third and final major catalytic element that will be considered in our brief overview of the renaissance also emanates from the world of ideas and perceptions. It was the radical new view espoused about the order of the physical world and the natural laws that seemed to govern it. The names of those who opened this door and thrust their ideas upon the world reads like a Who's Who of history. Nicolaus Copernicus (1473-1543) used mathematics to show that the earth moved around the sun and was not the center of the universe. This idea received vehement opposition from the Roman Church.[10] Francis Bacon (1561-1626) "called for a separation of reason and revelation. He believed this would have the advantage of facilitating the pursuit of genuine scientific

---

[7] Jones, p. 741.

[8] Jones, p. 742.

[9] Jones, pp. 743-751.

[10] Anthony Flew, ed., *A Dictionary of Philosophy*, (The Macmillan Press, Ltd., 1979) p. 72.

knowledge which, properly and systematically applied, would quite quickly transform human life for the better."[11]

Galileo Galilei (1564-1642) built on the work of Copernicus and so threatened the Roman Church that he was forced to publicly recant his work in 1633 while spending the rest of his life under house arrest. But in spite of his recanting, his belief that "the book of nature is written in the language of mathematics" carried with it tremendous power. The scholastic scholars of his day relied heavily upon qualitative thinking.[12] The idea of quantitative ideas was radical and, for many, challenging as well as exciting. René Descartes (1596-1650) concluded that mathematical reasoning was the only legitimate model for developing and advancing true knowledge. He challenged virtually all of the traditional presuppositions, even though many of them were restored by him in his own system, and he attempted to redefine and develop a new system of knowing.[13]

The real door that has been opened by this "new scientific thinking" was the beginning of a transition from the qualitative evaluation of the world, where concepts of God and values are important, to a quantitative evaluation of the world where "facts" are the important elements. This was shocking. It was like saying, "Stop ascribing the beauty of a gorgeous sunset to the power of God. It can be described in terms of dust, water particles in the air, and the angle of the sun. God is no longer necessary to understand it." The big question emerging now was, "How do you relate values to facts?" Or, "Do you need values where you have facts? Can facts replace values?" Sound familiar? Indeed, the same question still is being debated.

As time passed, the need for a concept of God seemed to become less and less important to understand the facts of the physical world. The men who opened this new door were, for the most part, Reformational men who believed in the Judaic/Christian God and the values associated with such a belief. For them, there was no conflict between God and the new science. But as time passed and generations came and went, God became an option in the minds of many. He was not necessary for an understanding of the physical universe.

In summary, the Renaissance was a new awakening of the creative potential of mankind. This rebirth took place under an um-

[11] Flew, p. 34.
[12] Flew, p. 120.
[13] Flew, pp. 83-86.

brella of assistance provided by the wealthy as they supported a growing intellectual community. From within this community of artisans and scholars came a new confidence in the ability of men to rule themselves if they would live under law and demonstrate respect for life, health, liberty, and private property while remaining tolerant of one another's theological beliefs. This should be practiced in a state where the laissez-faire principles are believed and followed. And the right to govern was to flow from the consent of the majority.

It should not be forgotten that while the ideals just described were worked out philosophically in England and Europe, they were experimentally undertaken in America and grew to their fullest maturity here. The ideas would have probably been stunted if so large a virgin territory had not existed in America for them to be tested. The R/R Ethic was most clearly seen in the States.

FORCES OF THE REFORMATION Now our survey brings us to the Reformational portion of the R/R Ethic. If the Renaissance elements reflect a surge in the confidence of the human potential for creative activity, the Reformational ingredients provided the justification, motivation, and direction for the R/R Ethic.

What was the Reformation? It was a sixteenth century religious reform movement that began within the Roman Catholic Church and ended with the formation of a number of protesting (Protestant) churches. These new churches placed tremendous emphasis on the centrality of the authority of the Bible in establishing practices for life and worship, and downgraded the authority of churchmen and their traditions where they differed from the scriptures. This type of reform was called for from within the Roman Church, but was initially rejected and those who persisted were cast out of the official structure. The roots of this call for reform may be seen in the work of such men as the Bohemian reformer John Huss (1375-1415) or Ulrich Zwingli (1484-1531), the Swiss reformer.

Our journey, however, will capsule the importance of the Roman Catholic Church in the pre-reformational period and the sweeping impact of the reformers, as embodied and symbolized in the persons and work of Martin Luther (1483-1546) and John Calvin (1509-1564). The combined ethic they espoused virtually cascaded onto the culture and replaced, in much of Europe, an ethic that had been hostile to human development and economic activity.

Church: The Dominant Force   The breakup of the Roman Empire was followed by political and social turmoil. Much of Europe was ushered into a period of genuine instability. What emerged were city states, feudal holdings, and the divided land of kings. These small regions were self sufficient and did not rely on economic or social interchange with one another. The one institution, however, which proved to be both unifying and stabilizing in the centuries following the collapse of the Roman Empire was the Roman Catholic Church. It remained an identifiable entity following the Roman collapse and was, by its nature, institutionally located within the boundaries of the majority of the independent "kingdoms." It was politically astute and over time became the wealthiest and most powerful force in Europe. It had represented the official state religion for the Roman authority and as such had been physically represented in every important cultural center. So it alone remained as a unifying and stabilizing minister in the shifting tides of Europe.

What was the mindset of this era? What was the driving concern and interest of the educated and uneducated; of the leadership and peasantry; of the strong and the weak? *The salvation of souls.* Economic activity was strictly subordinate to this interest.[14] To the twentieth century mind this is almost too much to grasp, but that was the fact of the day. The Church taught, forbade, sanctioned, regulated, and involved itself in every affair of life. The people feared the Church and loved it. They looked to it for guidance and protection. And the churchmen were viewed as holding power over one's salvation. The Church symbolized life and hope.

All of this direct and indirect control was exercised in conjunction with the name and authority of the local ruler. The two were most often allied. The rulers came to be tempered by the arrangement and the populace enjoyed a growing political/social stability. The power of the Church became such that eventually even the rulers came to fear its influence. The Church emerged the *dominant* force.

Not only was the main interest of the day the salvation of souls, but every aspect of life was understood to be part of one's personal existence so that every activity impacted salvation.[15] The world of business was considered a very dangerous place to occupy one's

[14] R. H. Tawney, *Religion and the Rise of Capitalism*, (New York: Harcourt, Brace and World, Inc., 1926) p. 34.
[15] Tawney, pp. 15, 16, 34, 35.

self.[16] Gains and profits were suspect and often branded sinful. The lending of money at interest was forbidden. Such activity could result in being cast out of the Church, resulting in eternal harm. These rules and ideas were both theological and practical from their perspective. Famine and plague had turned loose the forces of greed and the Church had moved to regulate wages and prices for the believed good of all.[17]

As towns developed and craftsmen grew in number, guilds were formed to prevent cut-throat competition. They regulated everything from the quality and quantity of the output to the prescription of the tools that could be used in the crafting process. The Church supported and participated in this activity by establishing "just wages" for the workers and "just prices" for the product. The entire system was designed to preserve the status quo. Profit making and social climbing were heinous ideas.[18]

The pre-reformation world was also the pre-renaissance world. The artisans and intellectuals were supported by the ruling class and the Church. The reformers were members of the Church itself. The rebirth of the classical humanistic ideas and the demand for a newly reformed church were both nurtured within the tightly controlled boundaries of propriety established by the Roman Church. The twin birth was revolutionizing. The reformers, however, were responsible for breaking the hold of the Roman Church on the populace. It was the protesting churches that provided the old concern for salvation with a new formulation and a new channel for expression. This reworking of the importance of salvation transformed its power from that of an economic brake to that of an accelerator. The resistant status quo was pushed aside and new avenues of personal freedom and expression were offered in exchange.

Movement Toward   Martin Luther and John Calvin were
Personal Responsibility both men who believed wholeheartedly
                         in the sole authority of scripture as a
guide for life and faith. They put no stock in church tradition that differed from the Bible. They taught that the institutional church could not bind a man's conscience. Only the Bible, in the hands of the Spirit of God, could do that. Furthermore, individuals were seen as being directly responsible to God and not the church. And

---

[16] Johnson and Krooss, p. 21.
[17] Heilbroner, p. 41.
[18] Johnson and Krooss, pp. 30-34.

people did not merit nor could they earn their salvation by their acts of obedience or good works.

These concepts separated Luther and Calvin from the Roman Church and thrust them into the forefront of the Reformation. The importance of the individual's personal responsibility and direct accountability to God (not through the church) coupled with the teaching of salvation by grace through faith (not good works) were shattering forces. The Church and its teachers were suddenly moved from the front seat to the back seat of importance. The demotion was dramatic and traumatic. Scripture was promoted and became the new driver.

The new ideas raised two questions, however, that demanded answers. The first was, "For what does God want me to be responsible?" and the second, "If I cannot earn eternal life, then how do I know if I am the recipient of God's gift of salvation?" Before we examine Luther's and Calvin's answers to these questions, we'll look briefly at another cultural force. There had been the wealthy and the poor for thousands of years, but now there was a growing middle class comprised primarily of those engaged in commerce. Money, credit, capital, interest, and profits were growing in importance and causing the church to lose its grip on a small but growing segment of the culture, because the Roman Church, in condemning this commercial activity, forced many of the emerging middle class out. One needs to ask if the Christian ethic espoused in the Reformation was an accelerator of capitalism, a genesis and cause of the market system, or merely a shaper of its character. The embryo that would eventually grow and become merchant capitalism (and subsequently industrial capitalism) was already conceived, coming to term, and awaiting birth when the Reformation occurred. This being so, the new Christian ethic is best understood as both an accelerator and shaper of capitalism but not as its genesis and cause.

Martin Luther rebelled against the concept of meriting your salvation by obeying the church and the canon rules which were set forth as guides for the regulation of one's life. He believed strongly in obedience, but as a *response* of love to a gracious and merciful God. He repudiated the idea that God's favor could be earned or deserved. This difference in spirit, attitude, and direction was one of the great gauntlets of the Reformation. This new emphasis spoke of the character and heart of God.

These distinctions in how one stands before God—under the

authority of scripture and by grace, or under an institution and by works—became for the reformers the keys to how one was to view life and understand his responsibility before God. All of life was to be seen in the light of God's free gift of eternal life (salvation) made available through the life and substitutionary death of God's son, Jesus Christ. All of life was to be a hearty response to this truth. Luther's mental anguish, that flowed from the tension between his self-recognized imperfection and the Church's teaching that salvation was obtainable through obedience, had tortured him for much of his adult life. The new Biblical understanding that salvation was a free gift to be received, removed the burden from him. He was free from guilt and wanted others to be free with him. He was so convinced of this truth that he singlehandedly "took on" the most powerful institution in existence.

Luther began teaching that all work was a "calling" of God. And people's response to this calling was their opportunity to show gratitude and give thanks. Being called meant every person had great worth and dignity. The cobbler, mother, silversmith, milkmaid, farmer, chimney sweep, sailor, and every other worker had a calling that was just as important as that of the monk, cardinal, pope, or king. All men should express themselves wholeheartedly through their work as children of God doing His work and bidding. This was heady and liberating stuff.[19] Suddenly hard work, sacrifice, and savings take on a godly meaning. They were expressions of gratitude and thanksgiving to God for His free gift (grace) of salvation through Jesus Christ.

The new and growing merchant-middle class was not embraced and endorsed by Luther either, however. He was still against the charging of interest (usury) and the "excesses" of profit making. He was living in an agrarian feudal society and desired to see many of the canon rules continued. It was the spirit of the rules that he wanted people to understand. Commerce was still a dangerous and temptation-laden "calling."[20]

The economic community was in deep need of having its behavior rectified or justified as the tension between it and the church grew. John Calvin and his followers provided the needed justification. This is not to imply that the Calvinists appreciated how they were being "heard" or interpreted within the commercial community. But the bankers and merchants welcomed Calvin's teachings on

[19] Max Weber, *The Protestant Ethic and the Spirit of Capitalism* (London: George Allen and Unwin, Ltd., 1948) pp. 79-92.

[20] Tawney, pp. 72-91.

the appropriateness of profits and the legitimacy of charging interest for the use of money. Their less than robust reception of his accompanying teachings on stewardship and the appropriate use of their profits to help the poor did not seem to bother their conscience as much as the profits gave them a sense of well being.

For Calvin and his followers, the "aim is not personal salvation, but the glorification of God, to be sought not by prayer only, but by action—the sanctification of the world by strife and labor. For Calvinism, with all its repudiation of personal merit, is intensely practical. Good works are not a way of attaining salvation, but they are indispensable as a proof that salvation has been attained."[21] The work ethic was born. Luther's expounding a "calling" and Calvin's concept of *successful* work being an indication of one's salvation were united in the minds of men to answer the two questions about their responsibility before God and how they could be certain of their having eternal life. The motivation and energy needed for a new experiment in the commercial world were now released.

Calvinism did not attack profits, interest, and competition. Profits were the fruit of a manager's labor. They were symbolic of his good work which reflected God's grace in his life and resounded to God's glory. Interest earned on money loaned the poor and needy was still condemned. But there was a new kind of money; money that was used and converted into productive capital, and interest earned on this was nothing more than an ordinary profit or rent. This kind of interest was not usury. The old laws regulating usury were good and should be maintained. But there is a new money, or new capital that deserved a different definition.[22]

It took the work of Adam Smith (1723-1790) to enthrone competition and the *accumulation* of wealth in the heart of entrepreneurs, but Calvinism had not attacked them. As stated, the stewardship of one's accumulated wealth was an important topic. As seen by Calvin, however, wealth was to be used for the help of others and not for bettering one's own personal standard of living. The concept of accumulating wealth in order to produce more wealth was not considered a good thing in its own right until two hundred years after Calvin. But the appropriateness of profits and wealth were established by John Calvin and his followers.[23]

---

[21] Tawney, p. 96.
[22] Tawney, pp. 102-112.
[23] Weber, pp. 108-128.

THE R/R
ETHIC

The Reformational/Renaissance Ethic (see Figure 2.1) has been called many names—"The Protestant Ethic"; the "Lockean Ethic"; the "Christian Ethic"; the "work ethic"; the "Capitalistic Ethic"; the "American Ethic"; and other such titles. Having so many names merely reflects the complexity and diversity of the elements that made up the old ethic.

The point here is not the selection of a title for the ethic but to state that the seventeenth, eighteenth, and nineteenth century workers and managers did overwhelmingly subscribe to an ethic whose ingredients were work, sacrifice, a calling, savings, responsibility, competition, roles by sex, concepts of equality/inequality, wealth accumulation, investment, risk assumption, and other compatible ingredients. And most fundamentally, it was an ethic based upon a view of God, the Bible, and mankind. It was presuppositionally a God/man ethic.

The nonreligious have on occasion attacked this ethic as a myth. The religious have at times been guilty of elevating it almost to the level of scripture. But whether attacked or elevated, it was not ignored and the mass of those in our culture accepted it. Imperfectly subscribed to, to be sure; rationalized and violated by many when it cramped their "style"; eulogized; used as a weapon of attack; and written about by thousands, this is the ethic of our heritage.

In the last fifty years, this ethic has come under attack and has been challenged by another heavyweight contender of fewer years. It has always had its intellectual detractors, but the masses stood by it until post World War II. "Who" is this new challenger and what are "his" vital statistics?

BIBLIOGRAPHY—CHAPTERS 2-3

Cassirer, Ernst; Paul Oscar Kristeller, and John Herman Randall, Jr., in collaboration with Hans Nachod (and others), *The Renaissance Philosophy of Man.* Chicago: University of Chicago Press, 1954.

Ferguson, W. K., *The Renaissance in Historical Thought: Five Centuries of Interpretation.* Boston: Houghton Mifflin Co., 1948.

Grimm, Harold J., *The Reformation Era*. New York: The Macmillan Company, 1954.

Ross, James Bruce, *The Portable Renaissance Reader*. New York: Viking Press, 1949.

Rupp, Ernest Gordon, *Luther's Progress to the Diet of Worms.* New York: Harper and Row, 1964.

Spitz, Lewis William, *The Renaissance and Reformation Movements.* St. Louis: Concordia Publishing House, Volumes I and II, 1971.

Tawney, R. H., *Religion and the Rise of Capitalism.* New York: Harcourt, Brace and World, Inc., 1926.

Thompson, Samuel Morrison, *Europe in Renaissance and Reformation.* New York: Harcourt, Brace and World, Inc., 1963.

Weber, Max, *The Protestant Ethic and the Spirit of Capitalism.* London: George Allen and Unwin Ltd., 1948.

Wendel, Francois, *Calvin: The Origin and Development of His Religious Thought.* Translated by Philip Mairet (1st ed.) New York: Harper and Row, 1963.

THREE

THE NEW VALUES

THE RISE OF THE NEW VALUES   The new ethical heavyweight that appeared on the American scene in post World War II as a mature contender was born during the Renaissance and nurtured during the industrial revolution. The big fight of the past thirty-five years has been for the ethical championship and the challenger appears to be wearing the old champion down. The Reformational/Renaissance Ethic is reeling in the corner. The old ethic comes on strong with a counter-offensive occasionally in the form of specific educators like Milton Friedman, or business endeavours, or a political action group like the Moral Majority. President Reagan's economic language represents a restatement of the old ethic. Words pertaining to hard work, sacrifice, productivity, efficiency, rewards, investment, and competition have been freely used. The battle continues to be waged. The presence and force of the ethical schizophrenia in our culture, however, speaks loudly and reminds us that one ethic has not yet successfully driven the other from the ring. And even if the new ethic should win, it does not embody the ingredients necessary to form an ethical consensus.

Look once again at Figure 2.1. The facing ethics on each side are vying for supremacy. Is work a means to a richer quality of life to be enjoyed in our leisure, or is leisure a time of refreshment in preparation for continued work? Which is the *end* value? This is how the individual parts of the ethics pair off. Of course, we have both work and leisure. But both cannot reign supreme in the value judgments of an individual or a culture.

Or, one can subscribe to a concept that is committed to the maintenance of sex roles while another perceives that such delineations are basically arbitrary, unjust, and unsound. The cultural impact of the two views is not to be minimized. Is there anyone left in our culture who fails to see that the redefining going on in this area is revolutionizing the world of employment and the family? The unisex movement and redefinition of sex-related roles is a significant part of the new ethic.

Every item listed as a part of the individual ethic has its own profound implications that touch every facet of our lives. To stand on one side of the conflict or the other is to hold a different view of ourselves as people. And two people who have widely differing ideas about what it means to be a person are going to think and behave differently in the ethical arena. There is hardly anything more basic to human relationships than one's understanding of one's self.

The old R/R Ethic was founded on a God/man view of reality. Men believed that they could only understand themselves and their universe in terms of an external spiritual reality. Even Plato (427-348 B.C.) subscribed to a form of dualism in which there were two worlds, a physical world of senses and measurement and another world (nonphysical, nonspatial) of ideal forms, where *prespatial* men had "experiences" with the ideal forms and models that set the standards for their physical experiences in the world. For Plato, there were ideal governments, ethics, and physical forms existing in the nonspatial reality. He did not build an elaborage metaphysical system of explanation concerning prespatial men and their pre-birth experiences but this concept was very much a part of his dualism.[1]

The R/R Ethic itself, however, was built upon the Judaic/Christian belief in a personal God who was creator, sustainer, judge, and redeemer. The predominant mindset in the West for hundreds of years was that an understanding of the physical reality necessitated an understanding of God's relationship to the world of senses and

[1] Jones, pp. 122-131.

measurements. This is even reflected in the fact that the history and science books used in American universities until the 1800s used interpretative and qualitative words such as "divine providence" (divine care and guidance) and "creator" rather freely throughout.[2] Well up into this century, the majority of people in our culture, both educated and uneducated, could not really conceive of something as complex as history or as simple as a summer rain storm that was not overseen and regulated by a loving Father.

Nevertheless, the power and force of a quantitative view of the world was on the rise from the beginning of the Renaissance. The gradual reshaping of basic assumptions took place so that our culture moved: from (a) It is unimaginable to conceive of anything physical in substance or impact that is not directly related to a sovereign God; to (b) It is possible to explain physical matter and events in terms of cause and effect which God has established and ordained by "natural laws"; to (c) It is most productive to explain physical matter and events in terms of the laws regulating cause and effect. (It is subsequently optional as to whether or not you may personally think of a deity as being related to the laws governing the events. Your factual knowledge will not, however, in this newer view be enhanced by such an association.)

The movement from (a) to (b) to (c) was gradual and carried out by humanists, philosophers, scientists, and theologians alike. In the fifteenth and sixteenth centuries, we saw the force and power of human reason unleashed upon both the physical world and the world of ideas and beliefs. Science came alive, willing to inquire into any corner of the universe. Philosophy began a walk to its outer limits and discovered the apparent limits of human reason. Theology found its doors flung open with demands for "verification and proof." The new field of psychology burst on the scene. Sociology appeared as a field of study. The "scientific methodology"; the "natural laws"; and deductive logic supplanted the old order of qualitative beliefs and faith. The 'new' became respectable and the "old" passe.

The observable character of the world (empirical analysis) and the creative, conceptual ability of the mind to deduct true knowl-

[2] John Higham, "The Construction of American History," in *The Reconstruction of American History,* ed. John Higham. (New York: Hutchinson and Co., Ltd., 1962) pp. 9-18.

edge about what exists (rational ability) gave birth to a new trust
in empiricism and rationalism. This tide went so far, in fact, as to
give rise to a counter movement that said, "No, you cannot understand reality by empirical measurement and rational thought but
can only understand it as you exist in relationships with people
and things in time and space." According to this view, what you
really come to know is yourself and your experience of the world.
This concept produced what is known as "existentialism," the
study of existence. This opened the door for the return of intuition
and mysticism on humanistic terms. And with this new ethic, the
Empiricist/Rationalist/Existentialist Ethic (E/R/E Ethic) the man
ethic, was formed and began to surge across our culture.

THE RISE   We twentieth-century Americans have a
OF SCIENCE   particular mindset that is so much a part
                      of us that getting a good understanding
of its influence on us is difficult, if not impossible. People who fly
on jets, drive automobiles, accept the idea and fact of kidney trans-
plants, turn on garbage disposals, and watch television cannot
imagine not living in a world of mechanical extensions and sup-
ports. What would it be like to have an unscientific mindset? This
is like asking the lady with six children to forget that she had ever
had a child. Our mindset is deeply influenced by mechanics. Ours
is a mindset that automatically sees and presuppositionally perceives almost any complex system (human body, galaxy, trees, etc.)
as being merely the composite of a lot of divisible parts that can
be adequately explained by "natural laws." Understanding and
function are explainable and dependent upon the "parts and
pieces." Human life is not merely *sustained* by the functioning of
the heart, lungs, liver, kidneys, brain, and other vital organs but is
soon *explained* in terms of the organs. This kind of thinking was
rare before the days of Leonardo da Vinci (1452-1519) and was
exciting and new to people in the 1600s.

From antiquity until the seventeenth century, people had perceived the world and all it contained as an incomprehensible mystery
associated with the prevailing concept of a deity. Then suddenly,
like a spreading wind, the human intellect began an enthusiastic
journey of discovery that fired the imagination and gradually transformed our culture's "world view" from that of a mystical unity
to that of a mechanical object which was understandable by human

reason. In England, interest in "the working of things" was so intense that "The famous Royal Academy (of science), of which Newton was an early president, was founded in 1660 and was the immediate source of much intellectual excitement. Indeed, a popular interest in gadgets, machines, and devices of all sorts soon became a mild national obsession. . . ."[3]

The people who had been awakened to the joys of exploring the physical world soon developed techniques of inquiry that we now accept as part of the scientific methodology. New words began to appear in the reports of men such as Leonardo da Vinci like experience, observation, test, experiment, analysis, causes, ends, and others.[4] The new vocabulary is powerfully suggestive. A common twentieth century word like "experiment" was loaded with excitement in the seventeenth century. It symbolized the testing of ideas, the ability to control and report, and the unlocking of mysteries that would yield to human effort.

The tools of mathematics and logic were propelled to the forefront. Measurement became critical to the functions of communication, control, and understanding. Logic is imperative for relating the parts and pieces to one another and for theorizing. Hypotheses became the stimulus and bridge to the other side of the chasm of ignorance. When natural objects or living things are broken down into their smaller component parts, a whole new world of wonder is exposed to human understanding. The complex is understood in terms of its parts. And the function of the parts helps explain the how, what, when, and where.

There were real benefits derived from all of this. As the world yielded its secrets, our life expectancy and standard of living increased. Man's inquiry benefited his fellow human and the excitement and human benefits proved to be economically rewarding. The stimulus to continue and expand the efforts made to further unlock the doors of physical knowledge was enormous. Science and its methodology were enthroned as the king and queen of progress. Its servants were measurement and reason. Its demands were for more progress and proof.

Today we are so immersed in the assumptions of science and enamored by its overwhelming success that few dare to question

[3] Heilbroner, p. 76.
[4] Jones, p. 593.

its weaknesses. Its own sacred code demands absolute freedom to be able to question anything and everything. Nothing is excluded from its purview. The point will be developed at some length in the next three chapters, however, that *the methodology brought to bear upon one's search for ethical truth will predetermine the kind of answer that can be forthcoming.* But let it be sufficient at this point to say that the rise of science and the development of the scientific method have had a profound effect on the growth and development of the new E/R/E Ethic.

REASON AND VALUES   By the middle of the eighteenth century, the problem of relating *values* to *facts,* while still almost two centuries away from being a problem for the average American on the street, had generated skepticism and confusion within the intellectual community. The empiricists who believed all true knowledge was limited to our sensory observations were on the brink of becoming genuine skeptics who questioned if anyone could really know anything with *certainty.* And the rationalists had maneuvered themselves into a corner where it was doubtful if they could control their own excesses and remain in touch with the world of *reality.* Both camps had much to offer, but neither could resolve the question of the place of values in a world of facts. The tension between knowing by observation and knowing by an act of reason was an old one that had existed even between Plato and Aristotle. But by 1750 this tension was at an all-time high.

It was into this intellectual ferment that Immanual Kant (1724–1804), the German philosopher, plunged. He believed that the two wings of knowledge (empiricism and rationalism) could be made to fly together in such harmony that a new understanding of knowledge could be developed. He succeeded and he failed.

Kant succeeded in standing with the empiricists and supporting their contention that observable reality is the most basic foundation block of knowledge. And he succeeded in showing that observations were insufficient to grasp all that might lie behind them; that perceptions could be deceiving; and that empiricism was inadequate to explain the knowledge of human judgments that accompanied most observations. Their theories were just too narrow to handle complex realities.

Kant succeeded in supporting the rationalists in their view that reason could formulate models of physical reality (or conceptual reality) before it was observed. And such projected reality could serve as building blocks for examining and predicting what the real world would really prove to be like. He also succeeded in showing that the rationalists could get far away from reality and construct nonsense when a real empirical world was not used often as a touchstone. Kant upheld and pointed out the shortcomings of both groups.[5]

But what happened to the big question, "How do values and facts fit together?" Kant drove home the point that scientific questions demanded a certain *type* of answer and that this type of category of requested information was not applicable when dealing with metaphysics (God), the unity of self (spirit and body), or the holistic questions about the universe. He told both the empiricists and rationalists they could not answer the question because their methodology did not fit the topic under discussion.

The question Kant set out to answer remained unanswered. He failed. In truth, the situation was now worse than ever. Previously men had failed, but thought they could succeed. Kant had now convinced them they had failed and should not expect to succeed. He told them the realm of values, metaphysics and theology were not open to the empirical, rational dimensions of the human intellect. Kant wrote, "I have therefore found it necessary to deny *knowledge* . . . in order to make room for *faith*."[6]

People now began to assume that *values* belonged to a category of thought with its resulting belief that was beyond (or beneath, depending on their attitude) the rational, intellectual formulations of the time. The idea of a "leap of faith," as the means of knowing God, became the new concept.[7] And this new way of "knowing"

[5] Jones, pp. 811-848.

[6] *Immanual Kant's Critique of Pure Reason,* translated by Norman Kemp Smith. (New York: Macmillan and Company, Ltd. 1963) p. 29.

[7] Soren Kierkegaard's "leap of faith" is a progressively developed concept and theme in much of his work, but it is not a specific phrase used by him. The introductory comments to *Philosophical Fragments* (translated from Danish by David F. Swenson show the concept to be pure Kierkegaardian, however (page xxii). In Chapter III of *Philosophical Fragments,* Kierkegaard develops the specific concept of the "leap" and its core importance (page 34). Then in Chapter IV he carefully defines "faith" and its importance in dealing with Reason, the Paradox, and the Moment (page 47). It is in his work *The Concept of Dread* (translated from Danish by Walter Lowrie, New Jersey: Princeton University Press, 1946), however, that the motivation for the "leap of faith" is developed. This is seen clearly in Chapter V, "Dread as a Saving Experience by Means of faith." Dread (despair), and the realization that Reason is incapable of proving God, serve to motivate the individual to take the "leap of faith" and by it come to a peaceful trust in the reality of God's atonement.

was gradually expanded to encompass knowing self and all values. This finally became known as existentialism—the personal development of knowledge resulting from relational existence. The new concept of knowing was swiftly carried into both the realm of philosophy and theology. Facts about the physical world would still be generated by the empiricists and rationalists, but these could not serve us when the deeper questions of meaning and purpose were raised. Only our existential knowledge—intuitive, feeling, and/or mystical—could inform us of values. The tools of progress developed by the scientific methodology were deemed to be incompatible with questions of value.

Then where does one turn? The answer furnished from 1850 onward by many philosophers and from 1900 until today by the majority of theologians has been to encourage this search for a nonprovable personal experience; a turning to, and relying upon, intuition; a personal feeling; or depending upon some form of mysticism. What was the bottom line of all this? The answer kept coming back from every quarter as a seeming echo—look to yourself! So humanism, in its many forms and guises, emerged in full force.

THE RISE OF HUMANISM

Humanism does not appear in a monolithic form, but simply put, it is human beings believing that they must look to themselves for care, comfort, guidance, help, solutions, and understanding in all of life's affairs, questions, pleasures, problems, and work. Our dependent, independent, and interdependent needs are to be met within the human family. People set the standards; their ideas become the values; and they evaluate and judge the standards. Men derive their authority from themselves; they are responsible for those things accepted as appropriate by men; and humans are accountable only to people. Mankind becomes the center of reality. Men are autonomous and sovereign. Man is "it"!

In varying degrees more and more individuals are coming to subscribe, at the "operating level," to the very broad definition of humanism just outlined. This is the rising outlook on life that is shaping people's view of themselves and their world. Growing numbers of people see this perception as the one in closest contact with reality and thus the truly viable option for themselves.

The past one hundred years have witnessed a number of individual and cultural forces rising to challenge, to ridicule, and diminish the support for the R/R Ethic. It has been weakened and the new E/R/E Ethic has been touted in its stead. We will now take a quick look at the two physical theories—evolution and relativity; a psychological concept—determinism; and the intellectual direction symbolized in the work of two men—John Dewey and Karl Barth; all of which have greatly supported and encouraged the rise of humanism. These theories were chosen because they were powerful ideas or shapers of thought which had great influence through others on the "man on the street."

The intellectual craze of the last half of the nineteenth century, among the natural and social scientists, was for the development of "neutral" facts in a manner that would let people explain human behavior and physical reality in terms of natural law within the framework of a mechanistic cause and effect view of reality. Science was making profound progress. This was reflected in the growth of applied technology. The understanding of physical laws was being translated into steam engines, sewing machines, farm machinery, and hundreds of other items. But when a mechanical cause and effect theory was plausibly put forth as an explanation of how man himself might have come into existence—evolution—the general cultural forces supporting the R/R Ethic began to stagger and disperse. If this theory were true, then people did not even need God to explain many aspects of their own existence. The psychological, scientific, and theological repercussions of this were profound and are well documented. But for many, an important need for God (the key of the old ethic) had been severely weakened. Humanism received a gigantic boost from the widespread acceptance of this explanation of man's existence. Under the weight of this theory, even if one wanted to hold to a belief in God, God at best was cast into a role that was impersonal and only involved to the extent of having established some impersonal general laws. The psychological weight of this possibility moved quickly to people at every level of the intellectual ladder. None could escape its pervasive influence.

The second physical bombshell landed in the twentieth century and was the concept of relativity. For the man on the street this finally boiled down to: things observed and thought about may not, in fact, be at all like what they have appeared to be. Or, to put it another way, you cannot be certain about what you know—an apparent contradiction. The level of confusion it created could be likened to having someone take a Polaroid picture at a birthday party and then, as everyone gathers to see it, have someone else

convince them that the man on the right side of the picture really
lived 2000 years ago and is actually dead now; the woman on the
left side of the snapshot is still alive but fifty years older than she
appears in the picture; and that only the person in the middle of
the picture is accurately portrayed. This is the state of confusion,
the state of reality, when looking up into the sky on a clear night
and observing the moon and a group of stars. Some stars may have
died but that new light has not yet reached us; other stars are still
there but much older than the light we see; and only the moon is
as it appears. Can we really trust what we see? If we change our
position and look at it differently, will this change the "truth"?
The phrase "everything is relative" is common everyday language
now. Is nothing knowable with certainty? That is the tension of
the twentieth century.

The success of science in the eighteenth and nineteenth centuries
also reopened for the twentieth-century inquirer an old conflict
that had existed between those advocating a view of "free will"
and those who believed in "predestination." But this time it reopened on the plane of humanistic psychology and not theology.
Immanual Kant had argued for the concept of the autonomous
man who was free and responsible for his own actions. The ordinary
citizen believed this, even if other philosophers did not think that
Kant had adequately defended his position on this issue. But over
the next 150 years, the mechanical view of the world, as seen
through the eyes of science, had once again raised the possibility
of everything operating from the basis of determinism—prior events
determine current events. The field of psychology had and has a
number of scholars who advocate that man's actions are best understood from a deterministic viewpoint. This view has been well
articulated and is used in this treatise, not because it has more professional followers than other lines of psychology, but because it
has, more than any other branch of psychology, permeated our
social fabric so deeply. Both in its correct form and distorted state,
it has challenged us all with the question of whether or not we are
really free and responsible for our actions or are actually reflecting
the effects of prior causal events.

Newspaper accounts of criminal cases often show the defense
using psychologists as expert witnesses who argue forcefully that
the criminals have been the victims of a poor family background, a
bad social experience, little education, and a generally rotten deal

in life. All of this is put forth as evidence to demonstrate that the accused are not as responsible for their actions as would be the more advantaged people. Other social areas are affected also. There is an unstated presupposition that accomplishing racial integration in education and legislatively acting to eliminate sexual discrimination in employment situations will, over time, reprogram attitudes that were learned, but exist without a legitimate basis of justification. We can determine; we can guide; we can construct; we can redirect; we can reprogram almost any attitude in society that is undesirable. These assumptions rest, to a considerable degree, on the acceptance of the hypothesis that man's destiny is determinable. When one subscribes to the view that man's destiny is determinable, then the belief that mankind is a creature under the sway of some form of deterministic reality must be a part of it.

During the reformation, men like Calvin and Knox argued forcefully for the concept of predestination. This involved God's certain knowledge of the end, from the beginning, and his plan for all men. What Calvin and others said on this was grossly misunderstood in their day and continues to cause problems whenever the subject is raised. Many interpreted it to be "double predestination," which is not what they, or the Bible, speak of. Double predestination means that God wanted to send so many people from his presence for eternity and planned to save so many who would remain in his presence for eternity. Predestination, not double predestination, rests on the understanding that God created mankind with the ability to have real choices—not required to choose good or follow evil—but that all men separated themselves from God in the exercise of their self will and by this have elected to remain absent from the presence of God for eternity. The Bible states that God ". . . desires all men to be saved and to come to the knowledge of the truth." (I Timothy 2:4). The teaching of predestination does go a step further, however, and says that just as men elected to flee from God, God has elected to struggle with men and save some for the purpose of showing his love and giving an inheritance to Christ. Biblically, predestination points to God's grace and mercy in the face of man's rejection of God's love.

Those modern men, however, who subscribe to some form of human determinism, while rejecting divine predestination, have substituted a form of natural, mechanical determinism or human elitism for the old theological concept. But in any case, natural humanistic determinism is one of the major forces currently vying for our allegiance.

In humanism, people look to people for their answers and not to an externally revealed truth. John Dewey (1859-1952) and Karl Barth (1866-1968) were both intellectuals who subscribed whole-heartedly to this philosophy. Dewey was an academic philosopher at Columbia University and a leader in the philosophical trend known as pragmatism. Pragmatism for Dewey meant that solutions to real problems should be sought, unencumbered by the constraints of "natural laws," "past precedents," and "dogma." He believed that what works is what is good. His confidence in "laws" (natural, physical, theological) was extremely low. People should discover truth through their own experience and not rely today on some-thing that worked for another generation yesterday. Dewey was particularly opposed to moral dogmatics. Values should not be guides to actions but should flow from actions correctly taken, as a good by-product. In this way each generation discovers those values that best suit their needs.[8]

Philosophers and theologians, according to Dewey's concept, would do well to be quiet on matters of morality. Like managers who fail to understand that refusing to make a decision is in itself making a decision, Dewey and his followers were not quick to point out that his "no value system" approach was a whole new value system. But this new value system (one must not teach old values) did sweep our country as this "school of thought" became the "in" philosophy for those involved in elementary and secondary education. A tremendous segment of our public education system came gradually to officially embrace the new theory—help young people discover their own values, but do not teach them another generation's set of values.

Karl Barth, on the other hand, fathered the widespread inclusion of humanism into the church pulpits. Many theologians were em-barrassed by their discipline's inability to respond cogently and conclusively to the rising claims, charges, implications, and ques-tions being hurled at them continuously from every other corner of the culture. While Immanual Kant had shown clearly that the scientific methodology would not work in metaphysics and theol-ogy, he had not articulated how reason was to handle these realms. How were the theologians to respond?

[8] Jones, pp. 949-965.

Some responded by abandoning the Bible as having any divine revelation whatsoever in it. In so doing, they renounced its authority within the lives of men. These men were called "liberals" and they concluded and taught that the Bible was mythology. Scripture was renounced as being accurate divine revelation given in a historic context of real events and was instead declared to be symbolic, representative, or allegorical. This group promulgated the belief that all of the Judaic/Christian "truths" were unverifiable and thus untrustworthy.

Barth stepped into the middle ground between those who adhered to the absolute accuracy and authority of the Bible and those who said it was completely mythology. He argued that there was just too much evidence supporting the fact that there had been a historic Jesus and therefore one could not simply discard the Bible as having no historical validity.

Barth claimed that the Bible *contained* historic and revealed truth while denying that it was *all* historic and revealed truth.[9] Who was to determine which parts were divinely revealed and accurate accounts of the past? Who could separate the truth from the illustrative; the reality from the embellishment? Each individual person had to sift his own truth, draw his own conclusions, and make up his own mind.

This newer position is known as neo-orthodoxy and dominates the world of Biblical theology today. Humans now are called upon to decide what is true and authoritative, and what is not. God has provided truth, but of a kind and quality that makes it necessary for people to find it. This form of humanism is in the pulpit and in the pew. What is merely a human concept of God and what has God accurately revealed of himself? The neo-orthodox answer— each individual must decide for himself.

[9] Karl Barth believed strongly that the Bible was inspired and was the revealed word of God, but he was not orthodox in his formulation of this. It was the "inner text" and not the "outward text" that contained the truth. The "outward" text—the written word—was not propositional truth (Karl Barth, *Anselm: Fides Quarens Intellectum,* John Knox Press, 1960, pp. 41-42). The "inner text" is really one's existential experience in living and wrestling with the scripture which produces a "dialectical theology." (Karl Barth, *Protestant Theology in the Nineteenth Century: Its Background and History,* Valley Forge, Pennsylvania: Judson Press, 1973, pp. 15-29, but especially page 22.) His rejections of the historic character of much of the Bible's record are clearly seen in his work *Christ and Adam: Man and Humanity in Romans 5.* This is seen over and over again in his tome *Church Dogmatics* and especially in Volume III, 2 which is entirely devoted to Chapter X entitled "The Creature." Part Two. G. W. Bromely and T. F. Torrance, eds., Edinburgh: T. and T. Clark, 1960.)

By the end of World War II, humanism had come of age. Our two hundred years of unabated physical progress gave birth to the assumption that man is perfectable (by evolution) over time and may help to achieve this end by his own self efforts—diet, education, social legislation, genetic engineering, etc. People, by necessity, if not by design, find themselves at the center of reality with no one to look to for assistance and guidance except themselves. The preservation of life *(one's own life,* especially as abortion, infanticide, and genocide grow in conscious acceptability) takes on greater and greater significance as the Christian teachings about redemption, salvation, and eternal life fade further and further into the background. In humanism mankind is left alone to resolve the question concerning the relationship between values and facts. There is certainly no cultural consensus.

THE NEW   To say there is no cultural consensus is
ETHIC   an understatement of fact. The old Reformational/Renaissance Ethic still prevails in our culture where people are committed to the historic Judaic/Christian understanding of reality and its concomitant ethic. The ethic, not the theological underpinnings, also still prevails, although to a lesser degree and in a mixed form, in those quarters where it has served well those who exercise leadership and ownership—our business community.

The new ethic, the Empiricist/Rationalist/Existentialist Ethic, has been growing in strength during the past thirty-five years. It has as many followers and probably even a few more than the R/R Ethic. Its bastions are the governmental bureaucracy, the judicial/legal system, the intellectual sophisticates, and the educational institutions. Its cardinal principle is that mankind must discover what is good and right while recognizing that this determination may be made in a variety of ways—rationally, experientially, relationally, etc.

As previously stated, however, not only is our culture divided concerning the choice of a primary ethic, but many more individuals are discovering that they have divided loyalties concerning the ethics. (See Chapter 2 for the outline of the ethics.) The more an individual finds the two ethics becoming equally attractive, the more personal inner conflict and tension will exist.

If one is not certain as to which of the two ethics most dominates his psyche, then taking time to consider ethical item number 8, Equality/Inequality versus Equality, could prove helpful. This is one of the two watershed items on the list. The other one, item number 10 (Thesis/Antithesis versus Synthesis), will be handled in the next several chapters. But a person's attitude toward *inequality* with its accompanying consequences, which is seen as a positive factor in the R/R Ethic's equality/inequality element and is seen as a negative consideration in the E/R/E Ethic's equality position, will go a long way toward identifying one's ethical leanings concerning these two major ethics.

Inequalities between individuals may occur at the intellectual level, the physical level, and through differences of individual experience. Benefits and disadvantages flow from these inequalities. Those people who find themselves to be advantaged will tend, as a group, to move ahead of the disadvantaged on the economic plane. The disadvantaged tend to find themselves, relatively speaking, worse off as the advantaged move upward and forward. A person's attitude toward the benefits gained through inequalities will typically reveal which ethic he or she predominantly favors.

The great issues of entitlement—am I entitled to something because of my contribution, effort, and merit or by the fact that I am a human with needs and rights—and the accompanying distribution of wealth are closely tied to the realities of inequality. Those who believe, as a matter of principle, that advantages gained through conditions of inequality are undeserved, tend to believe that people are entitled to many of society's benefits by right of their birth and needs. And, conversely, those who believe that advantages gained through inequality are deserved tend to side with the argument that people are entitled to their gains because they have earned and deserve them.

What presuppositions are held within the R/R Ethic that justify its holding that advantages gained through inequalities are just and deserved? Historically, the renaissance mind held that men were morally equal and equal in dignity. People were seen as being innately equal in worth before God and under the law. But the renaissance mind also held that it was natural (observed and reasonable) that some people would have certain advantages (inequalities) intellectually, physically, and by virtue of their personal experiences. This was the "nature of things" and therefore not to be forced into some unnatural form of accommodation.

The reformational mind affirmed that God was no respecter of persons in matters of justice and mercy and therefore under the law all were to be treated equally. They also treated inequality as God-ordained and *God-judged*–"For unto whomsoever much is given, of him shall much be required." (Luke 12:48). So physical benefits flowing from inequality were accepted as just and fair, and both the rich and poor were warned of the sins of selfishness, greed, and covetousness. The modern subscribers to the R/R Ethic either reaffirm these justifications, modify them for personal acceptance, or hold to them like a well trained "cultural bird dog" pointing to the scent of the past.

What are the assumptions held by the subscribers to the E/R/E Ethic that allow them to rest easily with the conclusion that advantages gained through inequalities are unjust and undeserved? The humanistic ethic has pretty much reduced the universe and mankind to an aggregate of atoms, cells, and cause and effect mechanics at the physical level. Birth is a function of chance and mechanics—sex, race, generation, intelligence, and physical ability. The humanist would not see God as sovereign and involved in the selective process as to who was to be a member of a particular race, in a particular century, with a particular intellectual ability. Political equality—equal protection under the law to life, health, property— is embraced by the humanist as it was by the renaissance man, but without the Judaic/Christian presuppositions. God's involvement, if it is assumed at all, is likely to be seen as passive—little or no personal revelation to be used as a benchmark and no involvement in the affairs of the physical universe.

So inequality is viewed as a "natural" occurrence, but one over which people have choices available to them for ameliorating its impact. Tornadoes are natural but men can build tornado shelters. Inequalities are real enough but are unfair. People have a duty to remove or at least reduce the consequences flowing from them. To this end, various forms of wealth redistribution have been undertaken through taxation and then selected social appropriations are made. In addition, legislative action may be undertaken to direct behavioral practices in both the public and private sector. The "natural" is seen as unjust. The humanist philosophy rejects the automaticity of inequality.

The R/R Ethic further believed that tampering with the "nature of things" would only set up a series of side effects that would be worse than the cure. The humanistic ethic believes in man's ability to control both the "natural order" and any man-created side effects. The old ethic understood man as a "fallen" creature with a "heart" problem requiring God's help. The E/R/E Ethic sees man as responsible for man's injustices and believes it is a waste of time to look for divine help. The differences between the positions are many.

The E/R/E Ethic is the rising tide. But so far the tide has not brought in with it an answer to the question of how facts and values fit together. Most scientists admit that the scientific methodology is not an appropriate tool for determining the answer to such a question when they are confronted with the R/R Ethic and its divinely-attached assumptions. Many in the culture, however, have a pseudo scientific mentality and do demand physical evidence and proof when confronted with questions about values. The neo-orthodox theologians have accepted the premise that it is the human burden to determine the correct values and apply them. God, in their view, has not spoken clearly or directly enough to expect much help from that quarter. Philosophy has fractured into groups of empiricists, pragmatists, rationalists, materialists, existentialists, positivists, phenomenologists, and behaviorists to name a number. Their voice is divided.

The basic problem generated for all of us by this cultural upheaval is one of being able to justify our answer to the question, "What is truth as it pertains to values and how do I determine it?" Philosophers and businessmen have exactly the same need. They both need a *basis* for answering the question.

FOUR

RIGHT AND WRONG: THE GODLESS POSITION

WHAT IS THE PROBLEM? When people begin asking themselves, "What should I do in this case?"; "Is it appropriate for me to propose that we follow this policy in our foreign operations?"; "Is it right to fire Jim?"; and other such questions, they are looking for answers that are built on "true truth" (definite, knowable truth about right and wrong) that will become applied truth. If Jim, the man just mentioned, is a 57-year-old regional sales manager who entered the organization ten years ago through a corporate merger and is not pulling his weight in the business, the marketing vice-president has a problem that needs to be solved. This is a value-laden problem. What does "truth" demand of a relationship between an employer and an employee? Does the vice-president merely examine the productivity aspects of the situation and conclude that Jim is inefficient and his replacement would probably generate greater sales and profits? Or does truth demand that consideration be given to whether or not the corporation fulfilled its responsibility to Jim, if any, and worked with him to give him an opportunity to meet the expectations his evaluators have of him. Did they explain their expectations to Jim? The very nature of the questions asked by the vice-president and the weight he assigns to each of them will determine the relationship of his ultimate answer to the requirements of truth—that his decision be "right." His questions will move him toward a right decision (properly applied truth) or divert him from the necessary considerations resulting in a mistake.

The particular process (selection of questions to be answered or intermediate actions to be taken) along with its accompanying assumptions (these are the appropriate questions and actions to guide us) that one employs in seeking a *basis* (standard) for truth will go a long way toward determining the findings and conclusions. Our assumptions, methodology, and process severely limit any outcome. The assumptions and methodology we bring to the process of determining truth have the same impact. As an example, if the scientific method is applied to nonphysical values (obligation, duty, or responsibility to Jim) it will automatically generate an agnostic conclusion (we cannot know what is right) because the methodology presumes testable, sensory related physical qualities that are not the controlling elements in making value judgments.

The R/R Ethic reflects a methodology for determining truth and reflects a host of underlying assumptions—God has revealed what is right and wrong. The E/R/E Ethic is based upon a totally different set of assumptions and its methodology reflects this fact— man must determine what is right and wrong. The two methodologies are presumptively different and give birth to the substantiation of two differing sets of truth. So we are confronted with an "old truth" and a "new truth." But what is the "true truth"? What should our standard be when we set out to determine the truth?

When ethical differences surface in a conversation they are soon surrounded by a defensive set of emotions. This is because people's concepts of reality are closely tied to their ethical views and when someone calls these into question it is like threatening to pull the legs out from under a house built on stilts. The whole structure becomes threatened. People do not just sit in the house and ignore the threat. They react, and on occasion not too politely. People will call one another's perceptions silly, irrational, anti-intellectual, unreasonable, and unprovable. People are rarely passive about deep, ethical differences when actual encounters affect self concepts, jobs, health, liberty, and a host of other aspects of real life. But both the R/R Ethic and the E/R/E Ethic are rational, intellectual, believable, and powerful. Bright people are not found on one side of the issue and the dull on the other. No such artificial division separates them. Issues like the generation of electricity through the use of atomic energy or answering, "How clean is clean air?" are examples of decisions rational people differ over.

A comment was made earlier that moving from one of these ethics to the other could be likened to experiencing a brain transplant because of the radical differences between the two. This becomes even more evident when one understands that the very categories of reality they incorporate are different. The R/R Ethic interrelates values drawn from the perception that there are *physical, mental,* and *spiritual* concepts of reality while the E/R/E Ethic sees values as emanating from a reality comprised of only the *physical* and *mental* aspects of life. One has three "working" categories of reality and the other, two. This is not to imply that those subscribing to the E/R/E Ethic are nonreligious or atheistic, although some are. It means that the divine impact is generally understood to be better or more completely discerned through natural observation than by special revelation. The divine is not central but "on the back burner" in the E/R/E Ethic. These differences mean that in some very important ways their process of validating and "proving" truth are quite different.

We are now going to examine how three different groups of people—one group will subsequently be divided to form a fourth group—interact with the two ethics. These groups' values are shaped by their differing views of the interrelationship that exists between the physical, mental, and spiritual qualities of reality.

MAKING VALUE JUDGMENTS   There are some very different kinds of *truth* in our culture. Some people hold that there are *absolute* truths that serve as our basis for value judgments; some hold that truth must be determined in the context of a particular situation; some hold that truth is always *relative* and represents a positional perspective; others claim that values can only reflect an *individual* understanding; and some *deny* the possibility of knowing what is right and wrong. This does not exhaust the concepts of the nature of truth but does cover the majority of options concerning the type or character of it. These very perceptions of the nature of truth emanate from our beliefs about what constitutes a holistic view of reality. Our polar positions about truth are reflected in the gulf that exists within our culture between those who believe in the reality of absolute values and truths and those who deny even the possibility of really knowing truth.

Let us look at the question, *"How do I determine what is true truth?,* through the eyes of three different constituencies—the broadly defined humanists, the orthodox Christians, and the neo-orthodox Christians. This question is central to any real understanding of ethics and values.

We will first define the three groups in relationship to their concepts of the *basis* of truth and then give several reasons for setting up these particular groupings. The definitions to be given are not altogether standard, but are helpful in focusing on the specific differences between the three constituencies concerning their view on the process of determining real truth.

The humanists' perspective on the search for truth centers upon the necessity for humans to determine what is real and true. In doing this, they must first conclude what constitutes a holistic view of the working parameter of reality. Does reality have three dimensions—physical, mental, and spiritual—or only two dimensions—physical and mental? Humanists are divided in their answer to the question. Once this is resolved by the individual, however, then he or she needs to decide how to best approach and conceptually encounter the whole realm of reality in order to be able to come to some specific conclusions about what is truth as particular cases present themselves. (How should I view discrimination?) People can approach the world as an empirical observer; they can rely primarily upon rational reason; they may believe that a relational experience is necessary to understand the true character of reality which is to be either discerned by feelings or intuition. Most humanists employ some combination of these approaches. Should the humanist settle upon a three-dimensional view of reality, then the spiritual dimension is conceived in a *non*-orthodox Christian manner—no special revelation—as to the deity's attributes, behavior, and positioning in relationship to the physical universe.

The orthodox Christians begin with the three-dimensional perception of reality, and hold a particular view about God's attributes, conduct, and relationship to people and the universe. The word "orthodox" is used here to connote the view, which was also the reformational position, that the Bible is the special, authoritative and true revelation from God concerning his character and attributes; the accurate account of his special involvement with a people for the purpose of providing an opportunity for all who would, to know and respond to him; an account of what is true about men's condition, needs, and possibilities for fulfillment; and a clear communication, recorded in propositional form, of what is right, wrong, expected and should be consequentially excluded from, or included in, people's *attitudes* and *conduct*. The orthodox Christian also holds that God is personally involved in using the scriptures to guide, lead, teach, transform, and comfort all who earnestly desire and seek a relationship with him in Christ.

The neo-orthodox position serves as a "half-way house" between the ranks of the orthodox Christians and the forces of humanism. No attempt will be made to try and define the specific point when one leaves the ranks of Christianity (in any classical sense of the word) and becomes a humanist, but when one rejects as truth, propositional statements contained in the Bible, then one has left the grounds of orthodoxy and has moved to the camp of the neo-orthodox. Rejecting parts and pieces of scripture as authoritative truth moves one methodologically to stand beside the humanists. It is now up to each human to determine what parts of scripture are revealed and true and which parts are something else. The orthodox Christians hold that God has given all of the Bible as completely reliable truth while the neo-orthodox believers perceive the need to determine which parts of it are true.

In summary then, it can be said that the humanists hold that there has been no special divine revelation to help mankind sort out the problems of relating values to facts or in determining right and wrong. The Christians say there has been divine revelation and it is recorded in the scriptures to guide people as they face the value questions of life. The orthodox Christian ascribes all of the Bible to divine revelation. The neo-orthodox Christian ascribes varying amounts of the Bible's contents to God's special communication, and the task of determining which part is revealed and which part is not is thrust upon the individual.

Why were the humanists, orthodox, and neo-orthodox Christian classifications chosen to tackle the problems of determining what is true truth? There are three important reasons. First of all, these three groupings cover the overwhelming majority of people in our culture.[1] By family upbringing, cultural permeation, or personal conviction, the vast majority of people would have little trouble with being classified as either a Christian or a humanist. Second, the Christian subclassifications of orthodoxy and neo-orthodoxy are extremely important, even if few ordinary citizens would be so careful about their personal classification. The old R/R Ethic found its justification within the teachings of the Bible. Now the church is itself divided along presuppositional lines concerning the Bible. The leadership of the neo-orthodox group began about eighty years ago to stand with the humanists in more and more situations and consequently the E/R/E Ethic found less resistance. The neo-orthodox group represents an especially fertile seed bed for the nurture of humanists within the walls of the very bastion of the old R/R Ethic—the Christian church. Third and finally, these three groups cover the necessary spectrum of positions without bogging us down in minutiae where the benefits gained from having more classifications would be questionable.

HUMANISTS' SEARCH FOR TRUTH

How would humanists search for true truth to undergird their decision to fire or keep Jim, our imaginary 57-year-old, unproductive sales manager? For purposes of our discussion at this time, we will assume that those who consider themselves to be humanists restrict their search for truth to the physical and mental dimensions of reality—two-dimensional humanists (2-DHs). This limits us at this point to the agnostic and atheistic humanists. They form one of the polar positions in ethics and for that reason alone are very significant. (The humanists who incorporate a spiritual reality into their thinking will be examined in Chapter 6 with the neo-orthodox Christians.)

The 2-DHs are confronted with the need, as is everyone else, for validating their perceptions of truth in the physical and mental

[1] Other minority groups in our culture such as Jews, Moslems, Hindus, Buddhists and others were not included because of the marginal benefit that would be derived from their addition. The phrase "marginal benefit" is used only to portray their marginal influence in our culture and not to disparage any inherent worth that they possess. The reformational theology that so heavily impacted the Reformational/Renaissance Ethic certainly had its roots in Judaism but the expression of it in the reformation was almost completely in the context of a Christian theology.

spheres of reality. How do they *prove* truth in these areas? The following table structures the problem we *all* face.

Area of Reality	How do Individuals Validate Reality?	How do Groups Validate Reality?
1. Physical	?	?
2. Mental	?	?

PHYSICAL TRUTH AND PROOF We will bypass the esoteric questions like, "How do we know there is any reality?" and start where ordinary, wholesome people have always started—we will simply *accept* that we are, and that we live in a real physical universe with qualities of time and space. Believing and accepting this self evident reality makes the individual's task of validating his or her physical reality descriptively simple. We accept that we have as part of our own physical being those characteristics commonly known as the five senses—touch, sight, hearing, smell, and taste. And with these, we encounter the physical world. So now we can begin to fill in our matrix as follows:

Area of Reality	How do Individuals Validate Reality?	How do Groups Validate Reality?
1. Physical	Use of five senses	?
2. Mental	?	?

No one knows if any two people find the taste of liver to be just the same, but normal people generally have no real problem distinguishing between different tastes, smells, sounds, visual objects, or the sensations of touch. Distance will blur our vision and time may dim the memory of what a rarely eaten item tastes like, but for the common, ordinary events of life, people in general have little trouble *proving* to themselves what they have just eaten, seen, or heard. General proof is accepted as self evident through the use of our senses. Yet no one will deny that there will be mistakes of identity through the use of the senses. Even this, however, does not destroy our overall confidence in their reliability. (Our occasional need for greater precision than the casual observation can afford will be discussed when we examine how groups develop a common proof when dealing with physical reality.)

From an accumulation of remembered experiences, people develop a whole array of likes, dislikes, preferences, and ambivalences. These, in fact, become so strong and occasionally emotionally laden that we even attach ethical values to physical objects and experiences long before we learn to attach monetary values to them. As an example, "Steak is better than hamburger," is a value judgment held by an individual who will eventually attach a dollar value to the preference. Philosophers call this a nonmoral value judgment—steak is not moral or immoral—and reflects a mere personal preference. But nonmoral personal preferences and moral motives and attitudes like greed, disdain, desire, etc. are instantly united. Suddenly personal preferences for nonmoral values (personal or national preference for oil) get loaded with moral values as people and nations begin to reveal their attitudes through their actions. Behavior is observed through the five senses and implicitly or explicitly evaluated through a value filter—personal interpretation. The evaluation process is automatic and involuntary.

Our five senses are employed in establishing the "who" (people); "what" (object or action); "when" (time and sequence); "where" (place and relationship); "how" (cause and effect) of our physical environment. These same senses do not, however, tell us the "why" of everything. And values ultimately *rest with* the "why" of life. The senses are data gathering but not evaluative in character. They are essential, as without data there could be no evaluation as we are constituted, but they alone do not tell us how to determine what is ethical or how to relate values with facts. Our search is for the ethical grail, the standard by which we declare something or someone to be good or right. Our senses identify, but do not evaluate.

In the physical realm, our five senses are the means of proving what is going on around us individually. But the communication of facts about the physical world, so that groups can have a uniform agreement or understanding about them, is a totally different matter. How do groups of people validate things in the physical world?

Suppose two people went swimming and one said the water was cold while the other said it was rather warm. It is obvious that their expressions, and perhaps preferences, are very different. So subjectively one can call it cold and the other warm. Getting a third party to jump in the water and report will not solve the problem of determining if it is warm or cold. We merely get a third *opinion*.

Opinions are not necessarily facts. Just because of such simple problems, over the centuries mankind has developed a host of *measurements* that would allow people to agree by referring their question to an impartial standard of measurement. Another of our questions is answered.

Area of Reality	How do Individuals Validate Reality?	How do Groups Validate Reality?
1. Physical	Use of five senses	Standardized measurements
2. Mental	?	?

People have developed literally thousands of physical extensions for their sensory mechanisms. The gallon is a standard measurement and we buy our milk and fuel oil with a sense of confidence when it is used ethically. We expect the butcher to keep his thumb off the scales and our speedometer to be accurate enough to keep us out of trouble when we are trying to obey the speed laws. We can now measure accurately for great distances into space or machine a piece of metal within a prescribed tolerance of a millionth of an inch. We "hear" far beyond the range of unaided human hearing. We see the bottom of the ocean without going there personally. Our senses have been extended into almost every corner of the universe.

But all of the wonder that this generates does not add to our ability to determine what is ethical or how to relate values to facts. We have made great progress in amassing facts about our physical realm of reality. But the universe is as unintelligible in the category of the "why" today, when approached through the questions and tools of the physical sciences, as it was centuries ago. Why gravity acts as it does and has the specific force that it does is still unintelligible. Physics and all the other sciences can and do expand our knowledge greatly in the "what," "when," "where," and "how" categories, but science is limited when it reaches the physical limits of reality. The "beyond the physical" is beyond science's capacity. Physical tools fit only physical objects.

Is there no ethical help provided by the physical facts when trying to decide if we should fire Jim, our 57-year-old unproductive sales manager? To answer "no" could prove to be a hasty and misleading conclusion. The physical environment affects people and their performance. The author knows of a situation where a man was promoted to a newly created position and after a year was dismissed for his poor performance. This same thing occurred twice more with other men. It was finally concluded that no one could successfully accomplish the task assigned in the manner prescribed. This could be likened to telling a distance runner that he will lose his track scholarship if he does not run a three-minute mile. The goals predetermined the outcome and resulting actions. What of Jim's situation? Have the standards of performance being applied to him been evaluated? Are there any particular physical facts affecting his performance? Jim may or may not get any help from a further examination of the facts, but facts are an integral part of our ethical judgments. *In any ethical situation, first get and check as many facts as can be reasonably gotten.* They have a tremendous shaping influence on our decisions.

MENTAL TRUTH AND PROOF   As in proving physical things, individuals validate the mental area of reality by *accepting* their own self awareness of the realization that "thinking" is simply something they do continuously and involuntarily. To be human is to think. The third blank in our validation table can now be filled in.

Area of Reality	How do Individuals Validate Reality?	How do Groups Validate Reality?
1. Physical	Use of five senses	Standardized measurements
2. Mental	I think	?

In the opening chapter, the point was made that an automatic and involuntary incorporation of ethical judgments is involved in all our thought and evaluative processes. When we are considering what is right and wrong, we will often, upon examination, discover that our thoughts are reflecting a past, present, and future orientation. Not only do we have a decision to make, but we also have *intentions* and *motives* which influence us and lead us to seek certain results. Motives are generally complex and ordinarily reflect both an "other" and a "self" orientation. They are subconscious sometimes and conscious at other times. People making business decisions cannot isolate the potential impact of their work upon their personal future. Motives are a driving force and our intentions are reflected in our means and goals. All of these are heavily laden with ethical considerations as they become part of our judgments to do certain things—in business or in our personal lives.

Validating what we think, however, does not *justify* attaching values to the decisions we make or the resulting consequences. To state that an intention, a motive, or a judgment is right or wrong goes far beyond the limits of proving and admitting that we have complex interactive components of thought. The contemplation of human motives is awesome but does not, in and of itself, prove that ethical considerations should be attached to them as if one motive is "good" and another "bad." That kind of judgment does not rest on the fact that we have motives and intentions, but on the presupposition that they are inherently ethical. This, in turn, rests on the assumption that people are moral beings. And this, finally, awaits verification of the belief that people are moral beings. Is this assertion true truth?

A major distinction that needs to be kept in mind is that there is a world of difference between quantitative and qualitative kinds of truth. Some people assume that to quantitatively describe a process of some kind will provide the key to the qualitative judgments about its rightness or wrongness. In a purely physical process, such as operating a conveyor belt in an assembly operation where "rightness" means the "most efficient," then such a quantitative approach will do. But as soon as we incorporate people on the assembly line and ask what is "right" and "wrong" in relationship to our treatment of them, then a qualitative element is included. *When a human is affected, ethics is present, and ethics is qualitative in character.*

Individuals prove to themselves that they think by accepting the fact that they are actively engaged in thinking. But how does one person prove that another is thinking or what they are thinking? In the physical realm the individuals use their five senses and the group develops standardized measurements to validate temporal reality. How does a group of individuals come to agree on what another particular person is or has been thinking? Juries, boards of directors, and others do this daily. We do this by citing the observed behavior or by listening to verbal expressions. When we observe a person driving an automobile or boarding a plane, we ascribe to them the accompanying thoughts necessary to bring about the action. Now the fourth space in our reality/validation table can be filled in.

Area of Reality	How do Individuals Validate Reality?	How do Groups Validate Reality?
1. Physical	Use of five senses	Standardized measurements
2. Mental	I think	Observe behavior

The observation of behavior, however, does not, in and of itself give content to the observer's concerns about accompanying intentions and motives. If the individuals acting refused to share their intentions and motives, then the observer is left with the necessity of either gathering as much additional evidence as possible, from which to make an inductive judgment, or to ignore the presence of these types of decision influences. In a court of law, people's motives and intentions are often sought, as the severity of the penalty is frequently affected by the presumed character of the motives. The qualitative elements give weight to our conclusions about the degree of "wrongness" or "rightness" in ethical judgments.

Quantitative facts and qualitative mental content are both considered important in most ethical systems. The basis of justification for an action (or character trait such as honesty) is dependent upon a set of beliefs that rest behind the sensory mechanism and reflect an interpretative process. It is important to understand that we do not see, hear, touch, smell, or taste *thinking*—our own or another person's. We see, hear, touch, smell, and taste their *actions* and consequential *results* which *mirror or reflect their thinking in part*. Only in part, because their motives and intentions are not so apparent. Seeing the reflected thought does not give one human the privilege of entering the mind of another for an exhaustive examination of that which surrounded the decision to act.

An executive may reveal all of his thinking but usually does not. He will state why he believes a big contract is good for the firm and his rationale for that perception. But he will rarely, in the corporate setting, also reveal what he hopes the contract will mean to him personally in the way of promotion, respect, salary, or other such considerations that are important to his own self concept. We are both exposed and hidden in our relationships with one another.

TRUTH THROUGH SYNTHESIS Having laid out the mechanics for validating physical and mental reality, we can now move on to explain how the two-dimensional humanists go about answering the question, "How do I determine true truth?" Their answer is always an incomplete and tentative answer, however, if they are faithful to the *process* they follow, *dialectical synthesis,* which will be defined shortly.

Let us quickly review the 2-DHs view of reality, their "proof" of simple reality, and then their basis or *process* of tackling complex reality and the accompanying ethical questions. The two-dimensional humanists are limited, by assumptive belief, to exploring the closed universe—no divine help from outside or within—and thus hold humans solely responsible for the determination of truth. There is a physical world of hard data external to us all and a complex sphere of the human mind, one step removed from our sensory perceptions. Since the mental process must be converted into "mirrored" actions by the thinker, the observer has a reduced degree of certainty about the specific thoughts revealed when recording and reporting on observed behavior. This is true for a number of reasons: (a) observations need interpretation to relate them to the initiator's mental processes; (b) the observer does not control the thinker; (c) constant, repetitive observations of exactly the same human events are difficult if not impossible to get; and (d) motives and intentions always underlie the actions and thus observations of human behavior are always only partial and *do not include the whole thought process.* But even with these limitations the process of studying the human mind and behavior has been carried on through the adoption of the tools of physical science, which concert, measure, and extend the five senses, to the study of the human mind (and brain). So the model or standard for determining true truth is the one used in examining physical reality which is then applied to all possible dimensions of reality.

By the beginning of the nineteenth century, the cutting edge of the intellectual community was trying to solve a problem that threatened the respectability of the concepts of those involved in the mainstream of the "enlightenment." Rational reason had come to the edge of its limits and people were questioning if men could really stay in touch with reality very long by relying exclusively on their rational abilities. Empiricism was also in trouble as it could be demonstrated that the physical senses could also lead one to false conclusions. The spheres of faith, feeling, and love proved to be immune to the tools of empiricism and rational reason. People were "getting out of touch" with themselves. Math and logic could not give adequate explanations. The senses could be misleading. There were too many contradictions. Even the respected philosopher Immanual Kant had declared that his knowledge had to be put to one side when it became time for him to consider things in the realm of faith. How could the newly enlightened man deal with the "why" side of reality? How could "facts" and "values" be unified?

Into this seeming dilemma waded the German philosopher George Wilhelm Friedrich Hegel (1770-1831). The people of the western world, until Hegel redefined it, had always conceived of reality as being explained in terms of opposing forces—opposites as understood in *theses-antithesis* logic. There was truth and there was falsehood. There was good and there was bad. There was right and there was wrong. There was black and there was white. The world was a world of absolutes.

What Hegel conceived of as a philosophical argument—the concept of dialectical synthesis (explained next)—became over time the apologetic basis for the field of science. And then, because of the great success of science, this new understanding of how you determine "true truth" became the assumed model for developing all areas of knowledge, including ethics. The revolution of thought that this new concept brought is the "brain transplant" of western civilization.

What is this Hegelian dialectical synthesis? In essence, it states that opposites (thesis-antithesis) are only apparent opposites but as greater knowledge and understanding are forthcoming, these apparent opposites will eventually be discovered to be partial and thus compatible (even identical) truths—forming a new synthesis.[2]

---

[2] Jones, pp. 872-873.

The "dialectical" is a new concept of the flow of logic. Opposites can be reconciled and one idea of truth need not be thrown out while the other is retained. The opposites are synthesized. The best truth from each is kept and a new and better truth is discovered. Good, better, and best truth are psychologically introduced. But the best truth soon becomes only partial or good truth all over again. (See the Thought Form diagram in Figure 4.1.)

When this new dialectical synthesis concept began to be applied to the world of physical sciences, where "laws" were not standing as "laws" very long because of the explosion of knowledge, this new philosophical concept fit physical inquiry very well. The insights of one scientist (partial truth or thesis) were discovered to be lacking as total truth (true truth) when totally different ideas

Figure 4.1   Thought Forms

A.   The Pre-Hegelian Thought Form

Thesis ←————→ **Antithesis**
(What we currently (A conflicting idea
hold to be true.) about reality.)

The solution is found in accepting one of the "positions" and rejecting the other.

B.   The Hegelian Thought Form

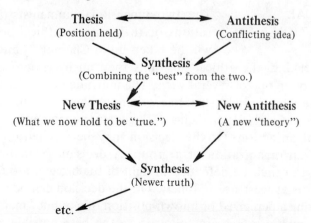

Thesis ←————→ **Antithesis**
(Position held) (Conflicting idea)

Synthesis
(Combining the "best" from the two.)

New Thesis ←————→ **New Antithesis**
(What we now hold to be "true.") (A new "theory")

Synthesis
(Newer truth)

etc.

Presupposes the absence of absolutes in all areas of knowledge. Truth is ever changing.

(opposing truth or antithesis) from a second scientist were discovered to be reconcilable with the views of the first scientist. The resultant new truth (synthesis) in turn proves simply to be the next new thesis (partial truth) waiting for yet newer truth (new antithesis) to be added to it so that a still newer synthesis can be formed. This is seen as an ongoing process of the never ending discovery of truth. Soon this theory of how you determine true truth was being applied to all fields of knowledge—physical and ethical. Its impact on the study of values was devastating. It only acknowledges humanly derived values.

In this new flow of logic—dialectical synthesis—where opposites are no longer viewed as irreconcilable (thesis-antithesis) but as constituting pieces of a truer truth, truth takes on a totally different meaning. "Truth" is something to be perfected. True truth is not possible at this point in time. Truth is relative. Truth is situational. Truth is tentative. Truth is ever changing. Truth is unstable. Who is to say what is true truth? Different people's opinions are equally valid. "You believe what you want and I will believe what I want." This is truth as many in our culture know it today. The views of truth just stated have become the humanistic formulation of truth. Humanists and others, as we shall see, do not accept the old process of determining truth. They reject ideas about final and absolute truth. They believe people must determine truth for themselves through an ever growing, changing, synthesizing process.

PRACTICAL APPLICATION The two-dimensional humanists' justifications of their various ethical postures will be taken up in Chapter 8, but practically speaking, the ethical positions they might choose can be settled upon in one of several ways. The individual decision makers can decide what is right (true) according to their personal values, and act accordingly. If challenged, the defense becomes a personal defense of an action. Or the decision may be reached upon the policy of an organization or a group. A decision carried out on this basis can then be defended in light of the broader group. The individual is at least not so lonely. Or, the decision can be reached by following a perceived or known position of a public "majority." Here the public mores are followed as the best possible action.

This concept of using a statistical consensus as a basis for resolving sticky ethical questions is growing in popularity in our culture. This is perceived as a good way to reduce risks of rejection. This approach does not look for a basis of action in truth, but looks for what is acceptable—a new kind of right or wrong.

BIBLIOGRAPHY—CHAPTERS 4-6

Barth, Karl, *The Word of God and the Word of Man,* translated by Douglas Horton. London: Hodder and Stoughton, 1928.

Dewey, John, *The Quest for Certainty: A Study of the Relation of Knowledge and Action.* New York: Putnam, 1960, c 1929.

Guiness, Os, *The Dust of Death.* Downers Grove, Illinois: Inter-Varsity Press, 1973.

Kant, Immanuel, *Immanuel Kant's Critique of Pure Reason.* Translated by Norman Kemp Smith. London: Macmillan and Co., Ltd. 1963.

Locke, John, *An Essay Concerning the Understanding, Knowledge, Opinion and Assent.* Edited with an introduction by Benjamin Rand. Cambridge, Mass.: Harvard University Press, 1931.

Sartre, Jean Paul, *Exisentialism and Humanism.* Translation and introduction by Philip Mairet (1st English edition). London: Matheun, 1970.

Schaeffer, Francis A., *The God Who Is There.* Downers Grove, Illinois: Inter-Varsity Press, 1968.

Sire, J. W., *The Universe Next Door: A Basic World View Catalog.* Downers Grove, Illinois: Inter-Varsity Press, 1976.

Tillich, Paul, *My Search for Absolutes,* with drawings by Saul Steinberg. New York: Simon and Schuster, 1967.

Torrey, Norman Lewis, *Voltaire and the English Deists.* New Haven: Yale University Press, 1930.

FIVE

RIGHT AND WRONG: THE ORTHODOX CHRISTIAN POSITION

THE TWO GROUPS   During the 1800s and early 1900s, the Christian community began to divide over the maintenance of a central, historic presupposition—the acceptance of the entire Bible, as originally recorded, as unerring truth. From the very earliest, the Christian community adhered to the belief that its scripture was absolute truth in all that it said. Martin Luther, John Calvin, John Knox, John Wesley, and all of the reformational leaders had no doubt about the Bible being divinely revealed, absolutely authoritative, and completely reliable in everything that it said. During the last half of the 1800s, however, a group of theologians emerged who challenged this presupposition. They approached the Bible with a whole new set of assumptions, hypotheses, and questions. They concluded that the Bible was not to be accepted as if it were one hundred percent true but that only some of it was to be seen as God's special and unerring revelation while other parts would be better understood as having been humanly derived. The new group of theologians freely admitted, however, that deciding what parts should be considered divinely inspired and which humanly derived was a matter of personal judgment. There was no standard by which such choices could be made.

It is not the point of this treatise to enter into this debate, even though it is still raging, but it is clear that the two sets of assumptions have a profound impact on one's approach, process, and determination of what is ethical. Those who subscribe to the assumption that the Bible is entirely revealed and completely reliable as absolute truth are called *orthodox Christians* in this work. Those who hold to the belief that the Christian scriptures are only partially revealed are called *neo-orthodox Christians.* The orthodox position prevailed with very little challenge for 1,800 years. It is also to be understood that this book does not purport to define who is a Christian. How much of the historical Christian teaching can be abandoned before one should drop the name Christian altogether is a theological question of great importance, but not the issue of concern here. The critical concern in this discussion would be if there were any movement from the position that accepts the Bible as being completely revealed (100 percent) to a position acknowledging any lesser degree (99 percent — one percent) of revelation. Any change, no matter how small, automatically moves people from orthodoxy to neo-orthodoxy because *methodologically* the neo-orthodox have placed themselves beside the humanists.

The entire Christian group, however, brings to our study a third dimension of perceived reality—physical, mental, and spiritual. And the significance of our subdividing the Christians into two groups is twofold: (a) we have a genuine historic continuity with the orthodox Christians of the reformation who shaped so much of the R/R Ethic; and (b) today we have a large group of neo-orthodox Christians in our culture who are a special class of humanists by virtue of the fact that they effectively remove God as an active third party in ethics and correspondingly place more and more emphasis upon the individual's need to decide what is ethical, apart from Biblical standards.

THE ORTHODOX   In their consideration of truth, the ortho-
SEARCH FOR TRUTH dox Christians begin with an entirely different set of assumptions about reality. Not only do they move from a two-dimensional concept of reality— physical and mental—to a three-dimensional view which includes

the *spiritual* sphere, but this additional dimension also shapes their qualitative understanding and evaluation of all three categories of perceived reality.

Ethics is essentially a *qualitative* assessment of the appropriate-ness of human conduct and traits of character and is tied to the deep questions of human meaning and purpose. The "Who am I" and "Why am I" of life underlie people's concern (or lack thereof) for their relationships and thus their ethics. The two-dimensional humanists are confined by their physical and mental categories to finding meaning and purpose within the realm of the physical and mental qualities of life. Their presuppositional base is grounded in one of two assumptions: (1) that learning more and more about the parts and pieces of the causes and effects of life will eventually bring them to an understanding of purpose and meaning; or (2) that simply experiencing one's own existence in relationship to the surrounding environment is our purpose and meaning. The ques-tion they must answer affirmatively, if failure and then despair are not to be the end result, is "Can quantitative data independently provide qualitative understanding?," or "Is life's meaning limited to experiencing ourselves in the environment?". *The quantitative physical dimension of reality or our existential experience are the controlling standards for qualitative ethical understanding for the two-dimensional—physical, mental—humanists.* (The three-dimen-sional humanists and neo-orthodox Christians will be discussed in the next chapter.)

The spiritual sphere of reality, perceived by the orthodox Chris-tians (OCs), is understood to have its own special qualities and quantities. Both what is not, and what is included in the category of the spiritual will be defined first. *Not* included is the concept of the human spirit. OCs understand humans to be composed of body and spirit (incarnated). The spirit and body are considered a *unity* and this is considered to be the normative state. The mind of a person (not the brain) is considered to be a part of the human spirit and is included in this book as part of the mental dimension of reality—physical, *mental,* and spiritual.

The OCs, when speaking of spiritual reality, are conceiving of a quality of "living beings" and "an existing other-dimensional real-ity" that are not subject to examination in its independent state through the use of the human's five senses. (The OCs "proof" of spiritual reality will be covered in the next section of this chapter.)

The very word "spirit" is used to connote an "other than physical" quality. So the ineffectiveness of the five senses in identifying it should be definitionally accepted when one moves into an inquiry of the spiritual sphere. This does not automatically relegate contact between the spiritual realm and the human realm to a non-existent or infrequent level, however. It merely says that the physical senses cannot be used to touch, see, hear, taste, or smell the spiritual. The external spirit, in this understanding, is left with the capability of contacting the human spirit or affecting changes in the physical universe that are observable by the human through the physical senses.

The OCs further conceive of the spiritual realm as hosting one God who has revealed himself in the person of God the Father, the person of the Messiah (Jesus Christ), and in the person of the Spirit of God; a multitude of God-fearing and loving angelic creatures; and a force of rebellious, God-hating angelic creatures.

In Chapter 4 where the OCs were defined, it was pointed out that they hold a particular view about God's attributes, conduct, and relationship to people and the universe as set forth in the Bible. God is conceived foremost to be *holy*—perfect in his being and actions—which becomes the *standard* and basis for all ethical considerations. The OCs compare their attitudes and actions with God's personal character. Both attitudes and actions are ethically important to OCs. The separation of the two opens the door for hypocrisy and duplicity. The OCs see ethics as a triangular relationship where God's revealed character, actions, and will are desirable to know as one seeks what is right for himself and for all parties affected. For the OCs an ethical principle is established: *when a motive and action are in keeping with God's character and, in a holistic sense, are in the best interest of all parties, then it is an ethical decision.*

The holiness of God is seen as the undergirding attribute of all his self revelation. Justice—every wrong has a retribution consequence—is holy justice. Righteousness—doing what is right, fair, and good—is holy righteousness. Forgiveness—the retributive consequence and alienation due to incorrect feelings, thoughts, and acts are removed—is holy forgiveness. Love—being committed to doing all that is truly constructive for a person without violating his dignity—is holy love. There are many other characteristics ascribed to God and all of them, too, are understood in the light of his holiness. But some of his attributes are seen by non-Christians to be in conflict with one another, such as justice and forgiveness.

How can a holy justice, demanding retributive consequences, be set aside by a holy forgiveness which removed the retributive consequences? Does this not cause irreconcilable conflict? The OCs understand these seeming conflicts to be reconciled through the life and substitutionary death of Jesus, who is seen as God himself coming in the flesh to become the unique God/man. His life is understood to have been sinless and the suffering he encountered prior to, and at the time of, his death satisfied the demands of God's holy character reflected in the requirements of holy justice. So justice is *not* set aside in favor of forgiveness, but forgiveness has been purchased with the price of satisfying justice. Mankind's indebtedness to holy justice is seen as having been paid off. Forgiveness has been purchased for all who would believe that God (Christ) paid their debt to God. Man's job is one of accepting the gift by believing (trusting, faith) what God has said about this whole matter. The understanding that salvation is a free gift of God, based on the finished work of Christ, and not based on works of self righteousness was the theme song of the Reformation and is still the understanding of OCs.

The significance of the OCs perception of God's love is that for them life becomes a *response* to a loving Father made possible through a loving Brother with the aid of the loving Spirit of God. The OCs want to respond and show their gratitude to God. God's favor is not deserved or earned but he is pleased when a life exhibits faith and love. They understand they are loved and desire to express love in return. When the OCs mind embraces the above understanding of spiritual reality, the Bible ceases to be understood as a book of rules or a list of "do's" and "don'ts." The Bible mirrors God's heart, his character, his love, his will, his willingness to help and share life with all who will embrace him. OCs are not opposed to rules and regulations. They do not object to written policies to guide and direct behavior. But for them life should be a response to God. Ethics—character traits and acts—is a reflection of their motives and actions as seen in the light of God's character. Attitudes and actions that mirror God's character and will are "right" and "good." Those that fail to are unethical.

PHYSICAL, MENTAL, SPIRITUAL TRUTH AND PROOF The two-dimensional humanists (2-DHs), as described in Chapter 4, and OCs both live in the same reality. The tools they use to investigate our environment are the same. The raw data they accumulate is the same. The quantitative facts (truth) are identical. So we quickly discover that the OCs use the same process for validating physical and mental facts as do the 2-DHs.

Area of Reality	How Do Individuals Validate Reality?	How Do Groups Validate Reality?
Physical	Use of five senses	Standardized measurements
Mental	I think	Observe behavior
Spiritual	?	?

All people must start with a simple acceptance of their personal reality and build from there. Our contact with the reality outside ourselves is through our five senses. In trying to communicate with others, we find it necessary to refer to some type of *comparative standard* or base of understanding. In its crudest form this may be simple expressions like "big as a house," "tall as a tree," or "sweet as honey." A fisherman might say the fish was as long as his arm. Points of reference and descriptions are needed when conveying any experience. But as the need for precision grows, we develop more precise standardized measurements like tons, pounds, miles, feet, hours, seconds, and other similar common denominators. This is all made possible by the fact that humans think and are capable of expressing themselves in words and actions.

With thinking, however, the ground rules shift dramatically. We do not see, hear, touch, smell, or taste our own or other's "thinking." As individuals we are self aware of our own thinking and automatically ascribe to others that they are also engaged in thought processes. We do not sensately see a person thinking but we do see, hear, touch, taste, or smell the consequences of their actions and verbal communications which flow from their thinking. But thinking per se is not subject to the senses.[1] People may *reveal* their

---

[1] "Thinking," not being subject to the five senses, is not intended to ignore the *accompanying* manifestations of the thought process that are measurable. Certainly the energy associated with thinking is measurable through instrumentation as "brain waves." And there is a vast amount of work being done in certain universities and elsewhere on the phenomenon of Extra Sensory Perception (ESP) where one person "reads the thoughts" of another person. But its very name indicates that it is not being observed through the five senses associated with any physical observation that is traditional in the West. (Many in the East speak of six senses.)

thinking or keep it to themselves, in part or in whole. The degree of personal revelation is a personal choice. Some people are very open and others are very private.

Because of these common similarities OCs and 2-DHs, as well as all other people, have little difficulty in agreeing on the majority of life's activities. Their view on medical techniques for surgery, the use of the newest technology in producing steel, the piloting of a Boeing 747, and a host of other important and routine matters do not differ because of our having dissimilar bases—two or three dimensional—for making value judgments. But there are a lot of places where the humanists and OCs *may* and often *do* differ in both their ordering and interpretations of the factual data and in the things they do that flow from their qualitative perspectives.

While the two groups of observers do interpret many facts alike, they also have important fundamental interpretative views that shape their ordering and acting on information. As an illustration, sociologists who approach their work from a purely humanistic perspective assume that the human behavior they are observing, as a general rule, reflects the "natural," "normative," and "evolved" state of humanity. The OCs assume that the human behavior they are observing, in general, reflects a "fallen," "separated from God," and "needy" state of humanity. Therefore, their interpretation and, subsequently, suggested active responses to observed conditions can be radically different.

The point to remember here is that the 2-DHs and OCs use the same tools and techniques for determining factual truths about physical reality and mental processes but have different interpretative bases for qualitatively ordering, interpreting, and acting on the gathered facts. Their perceptive differences are related to their exclusion or inclusion of the perceived sphere of spiritual reality.

How do OCs validate their perception of God's reality, attributes, and character as described briefly in the last section? They appeal to the rational, empirical, existential, and revealed spiritual forms of knowledge.[2] They embrace all four methods of knowing in a

---

[2] Stating that Orthodox Christians appeal to the rational, empirical, existential and revealed spiritual realms to validate their perception of true truth is not intended to imply that they completely discount or ignore the areas of phenomenology, behaviorism, positivism or other descriptive forms of reality. The latter are just less frequently referred to as separate concepts than the former as categories of description.

holistic system where each method reinforces the other three. They would state that they *experience* and *understand,* on a sufficient basis, God's self-revealed personhood and actions. (Validating groups in this case are made up of individuals with similar experiences and understandings.)

Area of Reality	How Do Individuals Validate Reality?	How Do Groups Validate Reality?
Physical	Use of five senses	Standardized measurements
Mental	I think	Observe behavior
Spiritual	Experience and understanding	Similar experience and understanding

Immanual Kant (1724-1804) tried to reconcile the rational approach to knowing truth with the empirical way and concluded that neither, either independently or in combination, could prove that ultimate reality was grounded in a "divine being." He ended with the belief that knowledge would not help his faith. Soren Kierkegaard (1813-1855), the Danish philosopher/theologian, similarly concluded a few years later that it required a "leap of faith" to deal with God. From these beginnings such expressions as, "Oh, you just have to believe," began to be heard in seminaries and later, the pulpits. And more humanistically oriented philosophers began denying the possibility of knowing anything of the spiritual. OCs reject these conclusions, expressions, and views. The Biblical view is that "faith is the substance (assurance) of things hoped for, the evidence (conviction) of things not seen."[3] "Faith" for the OC is grounded in substance that produces assurance and hard evidence that undergirds a deep conviction. The concepts of faith that hold it to be either "blind" or needing to be a "leap" across reality are not Biblical in their root. For OCs, faith is grounded in the rational, empirical, and existential relationship of the human with God. OCs contend that without all of the human capacities being incorporated in the formulation of an understanding of God, the God described by the Bible cannot be known.

Only a few important fragments of the logic underlying the OCs perception of God can be outlined here. It must be remembered

---

[3] Hebrews 11:1 (All Biblical references are taken from the *New American Standard Bible.)*

that rational logic is not the sole basis of their perception, but a co-equal supporting part of it. That God would be a spiritual quality (a nonphysical quality) is logical if he is to be above and exempt from all of the limitations associated with the parameters of the physical quality of reality. (Experientially Jesus declared God to be spirit.[4] Empirically the workings of the miracles of Jesus were ascribed to the Spirit.[5])

God, as a spirit form, could not be subject to the human's five senses of seeing, hearing, touching, smelling, and tasting. Therefore, "proof" of God must take another form than exclusively sensory physical proof. To insist entirely on physical proof of God's existence is tantamount to saying that "until God is not in the form of God (is not of a spirit quality but of a physical nature) I will not believe that God exists." That would be nonrational.

It is rational to accept that people think because we observe them acting. We observe the results of their acts. We hear their words describing their thoughts. But people do not see the actual thought processes. Because the human mind (not brain) is contained in a human body is not per se why people believe everyone thinks. We believe because: (a) people think (unobserved); (b) people act (observe their body activity); (c) there are empirical impacts on the environment external to the human acting (observable); or (d) there is a verbal communication (observable). For the OCs it is logical to conceive of God as a spirit, with an intellectual quality, who is removed from human sensory perceptions by just one additional step. Step (a)—people think (unobserved)—would be the same when the human desires to validate the spiritual. Step (b)—people act (observe their body activity)—would not be possible to observe when the human wanted to substantiate God's acts. When contemplating God, the first two steps, (a) and (b), are unobservable rather than only step (a) as in the case of observing humans. The human cannot see God think or act—no body activity to observe. But steps (c) and (d) are just as logical to apply to men's perceiving the reality and character of God as they are to the conduct of humans. The results of God's actions in and upon the physical reality would be observable in an empirical fashion— step (c), even if not repeatable upon human demand. And if God

[4] John 4:24.
[5] Matthew 12:28.

chose to communicate, it could either be empirically observable or mentally experienced—step (d). The human mental process is one step removed from being completely observable by a fellow human. The OCs perceive that God is but two steps removed from their human perceptions. But for them, to now be able to see God directly and observe body activity is not a logical or legitimate basis for disclaiming his existence or activities. It simply validates his spiritual quality.

For the OCs, it is also logical to understand that knowledge of God, of a personal quality, would depend entirely upon God's willingness to reveal himself in this manner, and that mankind could not capture or "find him out" through their physical and mental efforts. Being of a different quality (spiritual) places the entire burden for necessary revelatory activity upon God if humans are to know him. Therefore, apart from the special revelation of himself in the Bible and his continuing willingness to make himself known to those who earnestly seek him, mankind should not expect to know God and his nature and "heart" by their self effort. As people need not disclose their intentions and motives, or even what they are thinking if they choose not to, so God would need to act and disclose his mind if people are to discern his will. So the acceptance of special revelation is logical and rational for the OCs.

Logic has also been appealed to on the basis of the statistical probability of our experiencing life in such a complex universe apart from a "divine being" (Einstein's reason for believing in a divine being). But the OCs claim that logic (the rational processes) and the need for God's self revelation are only two pieces of what is necessary to know if one is to believe in the God of the Bible. For them there are also the empirical and existential dimensions that are necessary to understand God's true character and love. Logic alone may be sufficient to convince someone of the existence of a "divine being," but the OCs perception of a personally involved and loving God cannot be developed from logic alone.

So additional *evidence* is crucial to the OCs concept of God. Such evidence is essential if the points of logic are to be supported, and if the Biblical events are to have communicative content that will allow other rational people to evaluate its validity. Without such empirical (subject to the five senses) data, we would be left with noncommunicative feelings or intuitive judgments.

Much of the Bible is presented as the recording of empirical evidence (data), offering evidence of God's care for mankind as he has acted in special ways to help people by both: (a) revealing himself to bring about assurance, trust, and love; and (b) satisfying real temporal needs. Three empirical illustrations will be given. It must be remembered, however, that empirical evidence offered to a group of people in one context is reportable but not repeatable as is empirical evidence in a controlled laboratory sense. (Our own Civil War was a reality, but General Sherman will not return to re-burn Atlanta as proof of its first occurrence.)

The following is the Biblical account of God's provision of meat for the Israelites when they were hungry in the wilderness and doubted God's care and love for them at that time.

> "And the whole congregation of the sons of Israel grumbled against Moses and Aaron in the wilderness. And the sons of Israel said to them, "Would that we had died by the Lord's hand in the land of Egypt, when we sat by the pots of meat, when we ate bread to the full; for you have brought us out into this wilderness to kill this whole assembly with hunger . . ." So Moses and Aaron said to all the sons of Israel, "At evening you will know that the Lord has brought you out of the land of Egypt . . ." And Moses said, "This will happen when the Lord gives you meat to eat in the evening, and bread to the full in the morning; for the Lord hears your grumbling against him . . ." And the Lord spoke to Moses, saying, "I have heard the grumblings of the sons of Israel; speak to them saying, Between the two evenings you shall eat meat, and in the morning you shall be filled with bread; and you shall know that I am the Lord your God."[6] Now there went forth a wind from the Lord, and it brought quail from the sea, and let them fall beside the camp, about a day's journey on this side and a day's journey on the other side, all around the camp, and about two cubits deep on the surface of the ground.[7]

The very intent of the event was to call the Israelites to an attitude of trust. It was recorded to communicate the same message to future generations. A need was expressed; their leader expressed confidence they would be satisfied; a natural force (wind) was used to remedy their problem (blew in quail); and all of this was to re-

[6] Exodus 16:3, 4, 6, 8, 11, 12.
[7] Numbers 11:31.

veal God's watchcare and their need to grow in trust. OCs to this day perceive that the relationship between their expressed needs and God's providential answers to their requests serves as empirical evidence and substantiates their knowledge of God. The Biblical accounts and their own experiences serve for them as converging evidence of God's character and love.

The second illustration of empirical evidence is that of the recorded miracles. OCs accept the logic of miracles on the basis that God made the natural laws to operate at designed speeds within defined spatial limits, but free to speed up or slow down the time frame or alter the spatial limits at will. As an example, men make automobiles to run most efficiently at a specific speed (say 55 MPH), but are not offended if it goes 120 MPH or is parked. God is seen as having the same privilege with his "machines" and people. The apostle John records many miracles in the gospel he wrote and then said, "Many other signs therefore Jesus also performed in the presence of the disciples, which are not written in this book; but these have been written that you may believe that Jesus is the Christ, the Son of God; and that believing you may have life in His name."[8]

John offered the empirical evidence in the hope that people might see behind the "seen" and come to hold the same conviction about God that he held. OCs perceive that the same loving power is still being exhibited in their midst today. But the supreme empirical evidence pointed to by OCs is the bodily resurrection of Jesus from the dead. This event for OCs is the seal, the capstone, the strongest evidence serving as cement for their faith and substantiating their belief that all of God's promises given in the Bible are true and certain.

It was even recorded that the disciples who saw the risen Christ had trouble believing their own eyes. Thomas, the disciple who was absent when Christ first appeared to the others, declared that he would not believe unless he saw and touched (sensory evidence) the risen Christ. It is recorded that when he did see him, he exclaimed, "My Lord and my God!"[9]

OCs also often refer to common personal experiences (existential) like their deep conviction of sin (and sense of forgiveness in

[8] John 20:30-31.
[9] John 20:28.

Christ); their times of sorrow and the receipt of God's comfort; and their sense of anxiety in a situation which is replaced with assurance and peace upon communing with God. Reason and existential experiences tie them closely to the empirical evidence of the Bible which itself serves as the "benchmark" against which to evaluate all personal experiences. Their personal need, their personal experience, their logic and intellect—Christ commanded that people love God with all their *mind* as well as their heart—the empirical evidence of the Bible, and God's promised willingness to dwell with and help them, all serve to form a deep conviction, for the OCs, that the God of the Bible, as revealed in Christ, is true truth. For them, God in Christ is the beginning point for the development of any true ethical understanding. Christ is the standard.

TRUTH THROUGH THESIS-ANTITHESIS   In Chapter 4, the Hegelian dialectical synthesis was described as the process used by the 2-DHs to determine truth. In this schema, opposites (thesis-antithesis) are conceived of as being only apparently opposite with the belief that they will eventually be understood as contributing compatible or partial truths that can be combined to form a new synthesized truth. The new synthesis (formed from "old truths") becomes the new thesis which will soon be confronted with a new antithesis. These will be reconciled to form a new synthesis. This process is seen as on-going and means truth is always imperfect and tentative. Truth is perceived as changing and impermanent.

The above technique proved to be productive and useful when applied to the search for physical truth, but it also became the normative model in the search for philosophical, theological, and ethical truths as well. This has had a fracturing effect upon schools of philosophy and theology, resulting in the creation of many splinter groups. As time passes, there is less and less agreement within and between these groups, with the possible exception that more and more have concluded that true truth is unknowable. The OCs reject this conclusion.

OCs perceive of people as needing two methods for acquiring truth: one for the physical and another for the spiritual spheres of reality. But the OC's intellectual image was so damaged over the past 75 years by their inability to cogently respond to the wave of demands for "proof" that accompanied the rising success of science that their defense of how one can know true truth in ethical matters is not widely understood today. They became defensive and were virtually inarticulate about their own understanding of how you determine true truth. They have recovered to a considerable degree from this defensive posture now as seen in the works of Dr. Francis A. Schaeffer[10] and a number of others.

The OCs now recognize that when one is looking for truth in the purely physical sphere of reality, the process of synthesis along with its accompanying concept of tentative truth are essential. This is viewed as being completely compatible with the Biblical mandate for mankind to subdue and have dominion over God's created order.[11] Mankind in this context is expected to discover, learn, add to, and develop his knowledge. Synthesis is the appropriate process when atoms, chemicals, snails, and trees are being investigated. Their metaphysical origin, their "why," and their "value" are not, however, subject to the same form of inquiry.

Logically, the scientific and synthesis processes do not fit either the characteristics of the spiritual sphere or the necessity for special revelation, which is encountered when one considers the concept of a personal God. The OCs still maintain that when one asks questions about the qualitative values; the purpose and meaning of life; the spiritual dimension of reality; the metaphysical foundation resting behind the physical boundaries of our senses; the ethical dimensions of business; or the nature of God; then one is dependent upon the special revelation of God.

[10] Dr. Francis A. Schaeffer, an American Protestant theologian, has spent the majority of his mature life working with young intellectuals from all over the world who have been in search of the genesis of truth. Dr. Schaeffer has walked to the "ends of the streets of rationalism" with them; he has gone to the "limits of empiricism" with them; and he has let existentialism "run its course of unfulfillment" within them. And then he has offered them a view of historic Christianity as God's answer to man's quest. This work has taken place within the L'Abri Fellowship in Switzerland for the most part (there are other centers) and flowing from this work Dr. Schaeffer has proven himself to be a scholarly author. Some of his more widely read works are: *The God Who is There; Escape from Reason; Death in the City; The Church at the End of the 20th Century; He is There and He Is Not Silent; True Spirituality; Back to Freedom and Dignity;* and *Genesis In Space and Time.* He is one of several evangelical voices speaking clearly for the absolute dependability of the Biblical accounts of God's acts and statements in the history of mankind.

[11] Genesis 1:28-30.

In the field of business ethics, this means the OCs look for the *principles* and *standards* God has established and given in the form of propositional truth—statements that are absolutely true—in the Bible. Here synthesis is excluded and the process followed is one of thesis-antithesis. When the Bible makes a statement about people's attitudes and actions, these statements are accepted by the OCs as propositional truth (thesis). Any other statement that contradicts this thesis is considered false (antithesis). The propositional statements of scripture are understood to be reflective of God's holy and unchanging character and therefore become absolute standards or principles for guiding and shaping humans' attitudes and conduct.

OCs believe in absolute, unchanging standards and principles. Times and events change, situations are different, but the propositional truth that is to be applied to changing events remains the truth. Holding such an understanding does not imply that having propositional truth makes its applications easy. It does not. But the standards of what is "right" are given. The following is a passage from the prophet Isaiah and will be used to illustrate Biblical propositional truth.

How the faithful city has become a harlot,
She who was full of justice!
Righteousness once lodged in her,
But now murders.
Your silver has become dross,
Your drink diluted with water.
Your rulers are rebels,
And companions of thieves;
Everyone loves a bribe,
And chase after rewards . . .
Therefore the Lord God of hosts,
The Mighty One of Israel declares,
Ah, I will be relieved of my adversaries,
And avenge Myself of My foes.
I will also turn My hand against you.
And will smelt away your dross as with lye.
And remove all your alloy.[12]

---

[12] Isaiah 1:21-25.

Almost every line of this passage contains "good" or "bad" as seen by the Lord. It ends with his displeasure being expressed and his intention to painfully purify them—bring them back to what is "right." A few verses later, it is revealed that the purging will come because God loves them. What is the propositional truth of the passage? God is displeased that their silver is being mixed with dross and their drink is being cut with water. Their currency is being debased by those who control it. For two ounces of silver to be passed off as anything more is stealing. Any who steal—individuals, groups of traders, or those who govern—incur God's displeasure over such activity. The same idea is found in many parts of the Bible and never is it acceptable. Those who take bribes are singled out in the passage along with those who murder.

In summary, the OCs perceive the God of the Bible to be true truth. His character and conduct, as revealed in Christ, are the standards for all ethics. The propositional truths of the Bible reflect God's holiness. God's holiness is unchanging and therefore true truth is absolute.

SIX

RIGHT AND WRONG: THE REMAINING POSITIONS

ALL THE REST   The two polar positions have been presented in Chapters 4 and 5. The two-dimensional humanists—physical, mental— with their dependence upon the Hegelian dialectical synthesis process of determining true truth represent one polar position. The orthodox Christians with their dependence upon Biblical propositional truth represent the other pole. The two-dimensional humanists (2-DHs) have a primary dependency upon the five senses, reason, and feelings, or intuition for the determination of true truth. The orthodox Christians (OCs) depend upon the historic, special revelation of God to serve as their primary basis for determining what is morally right. The 2-DHs begin with man as the basic building block and the OCs begin with God.

The majority of people in our culture fall somewhere between these two positions. They can be described as either some type of neo-orthodox Christian (NOCs) or as three-dimensional humanists (3-DHs) who incorporate a spiritual sphere but one that is not compatible with the Christian presuppositions. The continuum constructed in Figure 6.1 illustrates these conceptual groups, their positional relationship to one another, and their process of determining "right" and "wrong."

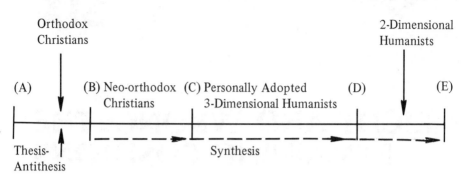

Figure 6.1

Allowing that each individual is unique, the continuum concept provides a spot for everyone. The general characteristics of "belief," however, are such that we may all be placed in some classification without ignoring the complexity or diversity of individuals and the group.[1] Moving from left to right on the continuum, the position (A) to (B) is the polar position of the OCs described in Chapter 5. Here ethical decisions are seen in a thesis-antithesis framework with Biblical propositional statements serving as the standard of truth. They are seen as reflections of God's unchanging character which makes them absolute truth.

Once you move to the right of point (B) on the continuum, the individuals, *to some degree,* will begin to synthesize humanly de-rived truth in formulating their ethical decisions. It is also not un-common to find people holding to absolutes in one area of life while allowing for flexible, situational, relative, or changing values in other areas. For some, this view goes so far that absolutes cease to exist as an intellectual option for them in any area of life.

On the extreme right hand side of the continuum (D to E) are the 2-DHs who deny the existence of a spiritual reality at all. This chapter will be devoted to a discussion of the positions held by the majority of people in our culture who fall on the continuum between points (B) and (D). Point (C) represents the extreme limit, as you move from (B) toward (D), of where one can still be clas-

---

[1] The reader could profitably reread Note 1 of Chapter 4 at this point. Everyone in our culture will not fit comfortably on the continuum as constructed, but the major-ity of those in our culture can place themselves within this framework without doing real damage to their sense of reality.

sified as a Christian. Their abandonment of the beliefs necessary to call them a Christian causes them to move into the 3-DH category. No attempt is made in this treatise, however, to define point (C). From point (C) to (D) the 3-DHs perceive that there is a spiritual reality and formulate their beliefs in categories that reflect a wide range of understandings that vary from deistic formulations to intuitive, mystical perceptions. The variety of perceived spiritual realities represented between points (B) and (D) will now be examined.

NEO-ORTHODOX CHRISTIANS

Neo-orthodox Christians (NOCs) are not of a single mind. However, people are placed in this category when they believe the Bible *contains* special revelation from God but deny that *all* of the scripture was given as true truth. They do believe, however, along with OCs that you validate reality as follows:

Area of Reality	How Do Individuals Validate Reality?	How Do Groups Validate Reality?
1. Physical	Use of five senses	Standardized measurements
2. Mental	I think	Observe behavior
3. Spiritual	Experience and understanding	Similar experience and understanding

Where NOCs and OCs differ is over the level of special revelation contained in the Bible. OCs believe that all of the Bible was given by special revelation. The group of NOCs who stand closest to the OC position believe that the Bible is special revelation where it speaks about God, faith, and salvation. But they do not accept it as true truth in those places where it speaks of geography, history, science, and other such nonspiritual subjects. This dissimilarity between the two groups reflects a deep and fundamental difference in their understanding and interpretation of certain historic evidence (empirical evidence).

The ethical repercussions of this difference are immediate and profound. The base and volume of special revelation is considerably narrowed and reduced by the NOCs. More and more questions of an ethical nature are now dependent upon men's judgment and God is understood to have given less help. The use of

thesis-antithesis reasoning is diminished and the dialectical synthesis is relied upon to a greater degree. There are fewer God-
given answers and more need for man-generated solutions.

From this initial step of disclaiming Biblical authority, the gap
widens even more as other individuals come to perceive that even
some Biblical statements about God, faith, and salvation are not
true. And finally there are those who believe there is very little
special revelation and propositional truth in the Bible at all. Eventually the character of God is only knowable existentially and not
at all by special, specific revelation. God's definitiveness diminishes
rapidly as the Biblical base is abandoned. The point to be gleaned
from this is that as the level of perceived Biblical propositional
truth diminishes, the level of dependency upon humanly-generated
answers increases. Eventually the point is reached where complete
humanism is reached.

HUMANISTS   Two broad categories of three-dimen-
                                  sional humanists who do not subscribe
                                  to a Christian view of God will be defined
and discussed. It must be remembered, however, that they too are
not homogeneous. They are also scattered all over the definitional
continuum within their category. First, there are those who believe
in a nonpersonal deity who is quasi-definable through reason and
personal observation of the natural order. And there is the second
group who believe in a nonpersonal divinity that is intuitively and
mystically known through existential experience. (Some of the
latter perceive themselves as part of the NOC's groups but they are
included here for discussion purposes among the 3-DHs.)

The first group is associated with the doctrine of deism which
holds that God is commended to the human mind by his inherent
reasonableness. There is no appeal to special revelation at all. After
God established the universe, he is understood to have removed
himself from it. The second group is identified with the teaching
of *pantheism* which holds that the divine is "in," and "a part of,"
everything. All physical reality is a piece, form, mode, state, or
condition of the divine. These two groups form the core of the
3-DHs. Most other 3-DHs simply hold positions that are variations
on these two central concepts.

Both of these groups validate truth in the physical and mental dimensions of reality as do all the other groups previously discussed. Where they differ is in their validation of spiritual truth; their qualitative interpretation and arrangement of the physical and mental data; and the resulting ethical judgments they make.

The differences between their processes of validating the existence of the divine are central to the various developments of the concepts of the divine nature, attributes, character, and actions. When our perceptions of the divine vary in relationship to these all important aspects of "being" and "doing," then the *function* of the divine is conceptually changed and our view of ethics is radically altered. How is this so?

As discussed in Chapter 5, the OCs perceive God as being personally willing to instruct, comfort, help, guide, and teach all who seek to know and have fellowship with him in Christ. Christ and his teachings—all of the Bible—set forth the perfect ethical standard and, in their light, people can examine their attitudes, motives, and actions. But even more deeply, Christ's life, death, and resurrection form the basis for understanding God's deep love and commitment to his children, which elicits a desire to please God—to live rightly—as a response of gratitude. From this perspective, ethics is understood to be a response and not rule keeping, per se.

The deistic humanists, on the other hand, perceive God to be an *observer* of men's lives but not one who is willing to be actively involved. To this extent, God is impersonal. He has revealed all he intends to reveal of himself through creation. From that point on, the human mind must, by dint of reason and natural observation, formulate standards, rules, guides, and principles or accept the necessity of having a variable basis for making ethical judgments.

People who subscribe to this view of God may conclude that he is caring or uncaring. They may hold to a view that there is no life after death or that there is an ongoing spirit life. These are qualitative judgments. Others perceive that God should be taken seriously as there are positive and negative consequences tied to observing or violating natural processes. Men and women debate over which acts and human traits are good in themselves and which ones produce good consequences. And people argue long and hard over whether or not ethics should be based on rules or determined under the circumstances. But the bottom line of it all is that, for the deistic humanist, there is no external standard—God given—apart from that which is available by observing the physical universe, reasoned out in the human mind, or intuitively known.

The pantheistic humanists may subscribe to the same general view as the deistic humanists but, for this treatise, those with a pantheistic perspective will be related to intuitive mysticism. This is done to cover the last major category of those who are humanists and subscribe to a spiritual reality other than what has already been defined. There are also many who think of themselves as neo-orthodox Christians while not subscribing to pantheism. But, from the standpoint of business ethics, they would either fall back under the ethics of the neo-orthodox Christians or remain here with the humanists.

As already described, a pantheist is one who believes that everything is a mode of the divine (the divine is the "substance" of everything). The divine is not transcendent or personal, per se, but is the incorporating element of all physical, mental, and spiritual reality. One's basis for holding this perception of spiritual reality is intuition. An intuitivist is one who has undeduced or spontaneous knowledge. The undeduced knowledge would be of a propositional form. This is propositional truth without special revelation from the divine or human time, space, historic groundings. It is believed truth that is independent of the previously discussed methods of validation. It is spontaneous knowledge in that it is unrelated to the sensory forms of stimulus. One is simply appealing to intuition, which some call the sixth sense.

Mysticism is not to be confused with mystery. Any unanswered question or unknown that awaits an answer is a mystery. Mysticism is used here to connote the direct experience of the divine in a noncommunicative manner—no verbalized messages or physical activity. The experience is a noncommunicative existential experience. One has a "feeling" that serves as a stimulus for thoughts. The divine is understood to be the genesis of the "feeling" by intuition and the experience is classified as mystical. The rationality of this is upheld by the fact that so many people testify to having had such intuitive mystical experiences, for example, while observing the grandeur of nature. From this type of experience, individuals develop a belief in the existence of the divine based upon their personal existential experience. There is, however, no claim to having any verbal communication. The communication is an intuitive perception.

What is the implication of this for business ethics? There is no claim of a divine verbalized communciation, so the individuals who perceive spiritual reality on this basis are left to doing what they conclude is right, based upon their intuition, feelings, logic, and experiences. Under this condition, humans are still left with the necessity of establishing and setting the standards of right and wrong for the qualitative dimensions of human conduct and traits. The divine has not propositionally given the standard. Humans must establish, by their own ability, all standards.

Intuitive mysticism is certainly not new. What is new is its growing popularity as a "post synthesis" alternative. As the acceptance of Biblical propositional truth (thesis-antithesis) has diminished and Hegelian dialectical synthesis has grown as the means of determining truth, intuitive mysticism has become much more widely accepted. The following quotation from the writings of Jean-Jacques Rousseau (1712-1778) illustrates the intellectual acceptance of this position during the period of the "enlightment."

> It is not in my power to believe that passive and dead matter can have brought forth living and feeling beings . . . I believe, therefore, that the world is governed by a wise and powerful will; I see it or rather I feel it, and it is a great thing to know this. But has this same world always existed, or has it been created? Is there one source of all things? Are there two or many? What is their nature? I do not know; and what concern is it of mine? . . . I see God everywhere in his works; I feel him within myself; I behold him all around me; but if I try to ponder him myself, if I try to find out where he is, what he is, what is his substance, he escapes me . . .[2]

The consequences of this concept of reality are even more pointedly discerned when we discover people pondering the massive complexities and problems within our culture who seemingly recognize that their own suggested solutions are inadequate and turn to find hope in the intuitive mystical realms of reality. A good il-

[2] W. T. Jones, *A History of Western Philosophy: Kant and the Nineteenth Century,* Volume IV, Second Edition Revised (New York: Harcourt Brace Jovanovich, Inc., 1975) pp. 3-4.

lustration of this is seen in the book *The Meaning of the 20th Century: The Great Transition* by Kenneth E. Boulding as he defines significant problems our culture faces and then offers some solutions as he sees them. Then, late in the book, he ends a chapter with this paragraph:

> Now if we look around us today to see what in man's experience looks like the foreshadowing of things to come, we may well find it in the experience of the mystics and the gropings of men in religion. It will be surprising indeed if man as we know him today represented the total exhaustion of all evolutionary potential. As our knowledge of reality grows so does our ignorance, and it will again be surprising if in this early stage of man's development he has exhausted all his modes of communication with reality. Even though, therefore, mechanism is the midwife of the great transition, the end results may well be a society specializing in spiritual experiences of a quality which we now realize only in rare moments of intuition.[3]

This is the perception of a great economist. This is not a theologian or a professional philosopher speaking. This is just one of many people who look to intuitive mysticism to provide the deeper answers to our questions of reality.

SUMMARY AND CONCLUSIONS   Practically speaking, where do Chapters 4-6 leave us? Is there any difference in the quality of the ethical decisions made if one is an orthodox Christian (OCs), a neo-orthodox Christian (NOCs), a three-dimensional humanist (3-DHs), or a two-dimensional humanist (2-DHs)? To address this question, a summary will be given of each group's way of determining "true truth"; their world and life view; and their commitment to ethical decisions.

Another presuppositional question concerning the will of people needs to be raised before attempting to answer the question just raised. It is, "Have you ever made a decision where you knew beforehand what was right, but willfully chose to do what you considered wrong?" This raises the ancient question of why people will, on occasion, choose the lesser good. Why would anyone ever

[3] Kenneth E. Boulding, *The Meaning of the 20th Century: The Great Transition* (New York: Harper and Row, 1964) p. 155.

will to do what they themselves rationally perceived to be less than the best? People from every walk of life face this reality of self expression all too frequently and especially when our personal desires, likes, preferences, wants, and wishes are actively present.

Without giving consideration to our volitional will, the whole area of decision making and its ethical implications is cast upon an intellectual plane that negates an examination of the depth and complexity of what we face. Decision making is not just passive, intellectual choosing among alternatives. There is often an active, strongly preferential, and driving *self will* involved in the decision making process. How do our four groups—OCs, NOCs, 3-DHs, 2-DHs—deal with the need for, and basis of, self control? Certainly our "self will" is an important element in the decision-making process. Until people come to grips with their occasional personal temptation to choose a lesser good in the face of an intellectually acknowledged greater good, they are unprepared to deal with the deeper problems of ethics. *Doing what is right is often much harder than knowing what is right!*

SUMMARY: TRUE TRUTH

OCs perceive God's revealed holiness to be the interpretative standard that definitionally qualifies all of God's other characteristics—his being righteous, faithful, just, kind, merciful, patient, good, love, etc. These abstract concepts and their perfection become concrete to the OCs through the Biblical accounts of God's communication and acts in history through which he revealed himself. He is good—his acts are good. He is just—his acts are just. God's attributes and acts become the standard for all human ethics. The propositional statements of the Bible are true truth for the OCs. They believe people are *enabled* to respond to truth and act in keeping with God's character by: accepting his love—perfectly revealed in the life, death, and resurrection of Christ; believing and trusting in Christ—what he said and did reveals true truth; and by fellowshipping with God—his Spirit uses the Bible to guide, teach, and keep spiritually safe the believers. God's desire for those who love him to be ethical is seen in the command, "You shall be holy, for I am holy."[4]

[4] Leviticus 11:44; I Peter 1:16.

The NOCs position is not so homogeneous. While the OCs accept all of the Bible as true truth, the NOCs accept only part of it as true truth. The "not so true" portion may be understood to be a reflection of the culture, a symbolic statement pointing to a yet undefined truth, or as a misperception reflecting error. NOCs do, however, believe there is some propositional truth given to us by special revelation from God. They do not necessarily agree, one with another, on which parts are true truth. That which is, is treated as a standard to guide them. The balance of ethical truth—non-Biblically derived—must be discovered through the dialectical synthesis process with individuals being compelled to make their own judgments about right and wrong. The information synthesized may come from the rational, empirical, existential, intuitive, and mystical realities. But any conflict that arises between the Biblical propositional truth and that derived by dialectical synthesis must be resolved by the human intellect. There is no standard external to the human that helps in the qualitative assessment of the ethical appropriateness of a decision once the synthesis process is entered upon. The human mind provides the standard. The NOCs have two sets of standards, some Biblical propositional truth and their self-developed standards. Where one standard ends and the other begins is a point of tension to be resolved by each individual.

The 3-DHs have only one standard to contend with, and that is their personal, synthesized, self-derived true truth. Their process for determining true truth may embody one, or a combination of, the following: rational, empirical, existential, pragmatic, intuitive, mystical, or other less widely followed concepts. There is no external standard of truth for the 3-DHs. Their personal perceptions become the standards. This is a fundamental difference between them and the OCs and the NOCs. The individuals with an external standard (Bible) find it necessary to check their perceptions against that standard and bring any deviations into line with the external standard or abandon it—thesis-antithesis thinking. But there is a "check." The 3-DHs do not have an external check. Their own reason or experience is the check. The internal checks the internal.

Even more fundamentally, however, the thesis-antithesis process of thinking, which has been standard in Western Civilization for thousands of years, is discarded even for their own internal mental checking. Synthesis becomes the habit. It is the new norm. When

the individual does settle on a value, and temporarily ceases synthesizing, the particular value is assumed to be true for the individual, but not necessarily for the world. Truth in ethics becomes
"personal" truth but not general truth. And even if "personal"
truth becomes the truth for the majority, that does not automatically make it true truth. Truth is no longer assumed to be certain
for the 3-DHs under any condition.

Everything that has been said for the 3-DHs could be said for
the 2-DHs with the exception that the mystical concepts must be
removed. There is no spiritual reality in their perception. This can
make a major psychological difference in one's perception of
meaning and purpose, however. Human existence, if contemplated
and carried to its logical conclusion in this framework, is reduced
to accidental chance, possibilities, probabilities, and other nonpersonal categories of understanding. But if life has no meaning,
purpose, or continuing hope, and that is the true truth, then it
must be reckoned with as it is when defined by any other group.
The outline in Table 6.1 summarizes the various ways of determining true truth.

**Summary: World
And Life Views**   Our concepts of right and wrong are in-
tricately interwoven with our larger understanding of the meaning, purpose,
and hopes associated with our being humans. The "Who am I?"
and "Why am I?" of life cause us to develop an understanding of
ourselves and the world. This understanding is our "world and life
view." Trees, cows, and frogs do not exhibit a concern about their
purpose and meaning. They seem to just "do their thing." But all
humans reflect on the deep, deep questions of life at various times
and then live out their conclusions or avoid them. Doing what is
right and/or choosing the lesser good both point to our view of
life. Again we find our four groups with differences, as would be
expected. Once more a continuum may be used to arrange their
perceptions about meaning and purpose—world and life view. See
Figure 6.2.

The OCs believe that man's being made in the image of God is
the key to the possibility of humans being ethical. Biblically, being
made in God's image means that men have the capacity for know-

Table 6.1 Systems for Determining True Truth

Area of Reality	Orthodox Christians	Neo-Orthodox Christians	Three-Dimensional Humanists	Two-Dimensional Humanists
Physical	1. Five senses 2. Standardized measurements	1. Five senses 2. Standardized measurements	1. Five senses 2. Standardized measurements	1. Five senses 2. Standardized measurements
Mental	1. I think 2. Observe behavior	1. I think 2. Observe behavior	1. I think 2. Observe behavior	1. I think 2. Observe behavior
Spiritual	1. Rational (examples) (a) God must come to man (special revelation) (b) God created and sustains (Miracles are reasonable.) 2. Empirical (examples) (a) Old & New Testament empirical accounts (b) Answered prayer 3. Existential (examples) (a) Guilt-forgiveness (b) Anxiety-peace (c) Comfort, teaching, etc. (a-c are Biblical norms)	1. Rational (example) (a) Genesis 1-11 are not reasonable (b) Man evolved and there is no "fall" or "original sin." 2. Empirical (examples) (a) Old & New Testament accounts (?) (b) Answered prayer (?) 3. Existential (examples) (a) More mystical and intuitive (b) Less communicative (personal feeling & intuition)	1. Rational (example) (a) No special revelation 2. Empirical (examples) (a) Only the "natural order of things." 3. Existential (examples) (a) Deist: no mystical; Possible intuitive (b) Pantheistic: possible intuitive and/or mystical	Denies the validity of the spiritual category altogether.
Establishment of Right and Wrong	1. Physical facts: Hegelian dialectical synthesis 2. Ethical values: Classical Biblical thesis-antithesis	1. Physical facts: Hegelian dialectical synthesis 2. Ethical values: synthesis and thesis-antithesis	1. Physical facts: Hegelian dialectical synthesis 2. Ethical values: Hegelian Dialectical synthesis	1. Physical facts: Hegelian dialectical synthesis 2. Ethical values: Hegelian dialectical synthesis

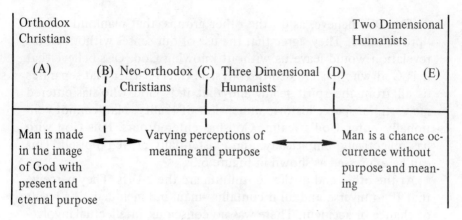

Figure 6.2

ledge, righteousness, and holiness.[5] Knowledge in this context means that people were made with the capability of knowing God—communicating and having fellowship with him. Then by knowing God, who is the standard of righteousness, people are able to make right choices. And finally, in knowing God and in making right choices, people separate themselves from what is bad and become more like God—holy. So for the OCs, being made in the image of God is a prerequisite for the possibility of being ethical.

The purpose and meaning of life for these people flows from God's "will" which is set forth in the Bible and evidenced in creation. God is the assigner of purpose and meaning just as men assign purpose and function to things they create. Biblically, mankind is understood to have been given the opportunity and responsibility for discovering, using, and managing the earth;[6] for reproducing and inhabiting the earth;[7] for living in a manner that mirrors God's character[8] and ascribing to God the awesomeness of his being and works;[9] for enjoying God;[10] and for delighting in all of life.[11] Life is considered full of wonder, meaning and purpose by the OCs.

[5] Colossians 3:10; Ephesians 4:24.
[6] Genesis 1:28.
[7] Genesis 1:28.
[8] 1 Peter 1:16.
[9] Isaiah 43:7.
[10] Psalm 37:4.
[11] Psalm 103:2; Ephesians 5:20.

The OCs believe, as do the other groups, that mankind cannot "prove" God. They agree that the use of our senses without God's revelation would leave us without knowing God. OCs believe that it is God who has crossed the physical (fact) barrier that separates us all from the spirit realm and that it is God who has entered man's time, space, historic dimension of reality. Man cannot volitionally enter God's realm. God has entered ours. It is God who has objectively, empirically, and existentially proven himself. This can be expressed as shown in Figure 6.3.

At the other end of the continuum are the 2-DHs. They perceive that the universe and all it contains—mankind included—is a result of chance or accident. There was no conscious, intellectual involvement in its formation. Impersonal energy or matter are the beginnings. So energy and matter are the beginning and end—the Alpha and Omega. In a final or eternal sense, life has no meaning. Its meaning is in the "now" or in the living of it. Meaning does not precede life or follow it except as it may provide some insights to succeeding generations. The "ends" of this life may cover a host of concepts from: having some qualitative or quantitative amount of pleasure, power, self expression and realization, truth, happiness, excellence, or to no meaning at all. This does not, by any means, exhaust the possible list of "ends." The meaning and purpose of life are not stated by a creator but by the individual. For 2-DHs, not only do people ascribe meaning and purpose to what they create but they do the same for themselves.

The 2-DHs understand mankind to be confined to a physical reality. There is for them no spiritual dimension. Their values are

Figure 6.3   The God Has Revealed True Truth World and Life View

God Has Entered Man's "Time," "Space," "History"

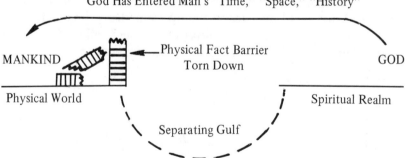

Figure 6.4   The Humanly Derived True Truth World and Life View

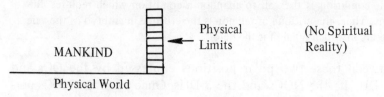

exclusively human in their genesis. This can be diagrammed as shown in Figure 6.4.

One of the most powerful 2-DH expressions ever made, in which spiritual reality was renounced, was made by Karl Marx who offered the scheme of dialectical materialism as its substitute. The following is an excerpt from his *Critique of Hegel's "Philosophy of Right."*[12]

"Error in its profane form of existence is compromised once its celestial *oratio pro aris et focis* has been refuted. Man, who has found only his own reflection in the fantastic reality of heaven, where he sought a supernatural being, will no longer be disposed to find only the semblance of himself, only a non-human being, here where he seeks and must seek his true reality.

The foundation of irreligious criticism is this: man makes religion; religion does not make man. Religion is, in fact, the self-consciousness and self-esteem of man who has either not yet gained himself or has lost himself again. But man is no abstract being squatting outside the world. Man is of the world of man, the state, society. This state, this society, produce religion, which is an inverted world-consciousness, because they are an inverted world. Religion is the general theory of this world, its encyclopedic compendium, its logic in popular form, its spiritualistic *point d´honneur*, its enthusiasm, its moral sanction, its solemn complement, its universal basis of consolation and justification. It is the fantastic realization of the human being because the human being has attained no true reality. Thus, the struggle against religion is indirectly the struggle against the world of which religion is the spiritual aroma.

The wretchedness of religion is at once an expression of and a protest against real wretchedness. Religion is the sigh of the oppressed creature, the heart of a heartless world and the soul of soulless conditions. It is the opium of the people.

The abolition of religion as the illusory happiness of the people is a

---

[12] Karl Marx, *Critique of Hegel's "Philosophy of Right,"* Joseph O'Malley, ed. (New York: Cambridge University Press, 1970), p. 131.

demand for their true happiness. The call to abandon illusions about their condition is the call to abandon a condition which requires illusions. Thus, the critique of religion is the critique in embryo of the vale of tears of which religion is the halo."

Between these two polar positions expressed by the OCs and the 2-DHs lie the NOCs and the 3-DHs. Once again the NOCs perceive that meaning and purpose flow from God but its discovery is partially God-given and partially to be man-determined. They straddle the two positions in the belief that there is some special revelation of God's "will" and purposes for mankind. They look to God and to themselves. The Bible may be of some help but most look to a *moment* of feeling, an existential experience with God or a mystical encounter to validate their source of true truth. They perceive that man's encounter with God must be in the realm of the nonrational and nonempirical. It is a kind of "leap of faith." The NOCs concept is diagrammed in Figure 6.5.

The 3-DHs believe in some concept of the divine but do not subscribe to any special revelation. God for them is deistic or the divine is pantheistic. Therefore, life's purpose and meaning are to be deduced from logic, empirical observations, and/or existential experiences. The 3-DH's world and life view will be a personal mix incorporating the "ends" mentioned previously for the 2-DHs, blended with, and tempered by, a view of the spiritual. The range of possibilities is enormous. For them, the divine is real but values must be humanly derived because humans cannot cross the physical (fact) barrier and the divine has not, according to them, entered man's world—deism. This position is diagrammed in Figure 6.6.

Figure 6.5   The God/Man Intuitively, Mystically Derived True Truth
World and Life View

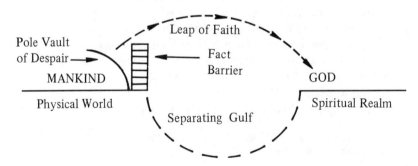

Figure 6.6 The Humanly Derived True Truth World and Life View

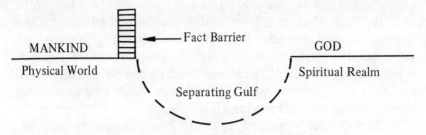

COMMITMENT TO ETHICAL DECISIONS

Our world and life view is affected by our view of true truth. Is our commitment to being ethical affected by our view of truth and our world and life view? Does one or the other of our groups have a special handle on dealing with morality and the lurking problem of our being tempted to choose the lesser good by which we may violate our own knowledge of what is right?

The commitment to doing what is right is not confined to any group. Individuals in any of the groups may carry a genuine burden for doing what is right and avoiding what is wrong. Each of the groups have had strong moral leaders committed to their cause. Would any individual in one group state that another group is more right or ethical and remain committed to their position? Hardly.

So at the individual level, one group does not have the kind of corner on the ethical market that will allow them to persuade all others to join them. Agreements and disagreements abound *within* and *between* the different groups. To be committed to an understanding of truth means that all who are of that persuasion believe the others are wrong or they are waiting for a new synthesis which, from their perspective, will probably bring the variant groups closer to their own viewpoint. Varying groups exist and exhibit their differences and inabilities to convince others of their own position. No human can bring about what our coming into existence did not achieve, and that is to provide everyone with the same perception of true truth.

The volitional will, the self-will, the willful commitment to "my desires," "my way" is experienced by every human in each of our four groups. The OCs say that only God's will is normative and that "free will" for men means their ability to choose and follow God's will. They believe that "free will" was rendered inoperable with the "fall of all in Adam" and that volitional self-will became the norm for all men after the "fall." The possibility of growing in self-control—control of the volitional self-will—and of regaining some level of "free will" is, as perceived by the OCs, made real by returning to fellowship with God through which true knowledge, righteousness, and holiness are affected.

While OCs talk of a commitment to Jesus, humanists speak of a commitment to a moral position. The 3-DHs and the 2-DHs believe that people can be helped to choose the moral best over a lesser good through education, exposure to the benefits and consequences of moral actions, and encouragement. They perceive that the problem of choosing the lesser good is a break in the sense of duty;[13] psychologically connected with present and future benefits, where the present ones seem stronger than the future ones because of their nearness;[14] a function of our present circumstances and our descriptive perception of just what is good:[15] or other such concepts. But whatever the concept, for the humanists there is no "fall of man." The "free will" of men was not rendered inoperable but is seen in the self-will of men. God's will (for the 3-DHs) is for men to discover right and wrong and not to be given some external standard by special revelation.

CONCLUSION   Some things are clear. We have four clearly distinctive perceptions about the divine. There is the God of Christ. There is the deistic God. There is the pantheistic concept of the divine. There is the concept that there is no divine reality. There are four clear differences about how you validate the divine: God has entered into the time and space dimensions of our reality by speaking and acting so that people of all periods can know, seek, and have fellowship with him; God is only knowable through the applications of reason and the observation of the natural universe; the divine is existentially realized through intuitive mysticism; and there is no validation.

[13] Jones, p. 70-72.
[14] Jones, Volume III. *Hobbes to Hume*, pp. 260-261.
[15] Jones, Volume V, *The Twentieth Century to Wittgenstein and Sartre*, pp. 290-291.

Quantitatively the four groups of people all have the same physical universe to live in. They all have the same five senses with which to explore the universe. They all have a mind with reasoning ability. They all observe one another's behavior and listen to the words from each other's mouths. They can agree on observable facts.

Qualitatively they are very different. Their bases of determining, and standard for evaluating ethical truths are different. Their world and life views are different. Their understanding of human purpose and meaning are very different. They interpret human nature differently. They put life together differently.

One way to demonstrate this concretely is to assume that everyone has a Box A as shown in Figure 6.7.

Box A and Box B are the same except for *emphasis.* Box A and Box C are the same except for *emphasis.* But Box B and Box C are facing in different directions. They are different views of the same raw data. The analogy must not be pushed too far because the differences between our OCs, NOCs, 3-DHs, and 2-DHs are not created by optical illusions. Their differences are qualitative, perceptual, and interpretative. And the most basic beginning ingredient for the individual is "self."

We humans are finite. We possess self-awareness to a high degree. We are the ones who ask, "Who am I?" and "Why am I?" The

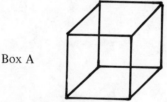

Box A

The basic ingredients of Box A can be interpreted in radically different ways. Boxes B and C are Box A interpreted differently.

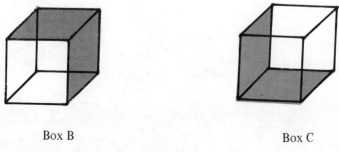

Box B   Box C

Figure 6.7

perceived genesis, meaning, and purpose of "self" are at the center-most point of our identity and understanding of reality. The perceived character of the divine or the emptiness of "chance" form the basis of ethics. We are all stimulated by our surroundings and involuntarily find ourselves repeatedly making qualitative judgments about things, people, and actions.

Our past three chapters have highlighted the bases and significant reasons for our differences which have produced the ethical schizophrenia our culture is experiencing. The older ethic and the newer ethic reflect the changes in our perceptive base about meaning and purpose, self and others, and God.

We want to turn now to an examination of the ethical "highways" people travel on when they speak and reveal their perceptions of true truth. When we are listening to others speak, we need to learn how to determine where they are coming from and where they are going ethically. These ethical highways are the routes over which people deliver their particular brand of true truth.

SEVEN

THE ETHICAL HIGHWAYS

The ethical backseat drivers referred to in the opening paragraph of the book may get excited at almost any time and for a variety of reasons begin shouting ethical directions at those who lead our organizations. This usually occurs because there are differences of opinion over a proposed or already taken action. And when this is the case, you can be assured that the parties also will disagree on some basic assumptions that constitute the undergirding rationale for the decision. For example, they may not like the basic "ethical highway" being traveled—may approach a problem differently: from a normative direction ("it is good in itself") or from a consequential direction ("it results in a good consequence"). They may not like the "style of driving"—they may not like having "rules" to guide them. They may be looking for different "landmarks"—there are *moral* and *nonmoral* values resting side by side in most business decisions. They may have different reasons for "taking the trip"—what is the basis for declaring that the "end" is good? And finally, they may demand a *justification* for everything—the big and final "why" or "who says?" (Chapter 8 will be devoted to this last question.)

We are indebted to the philosophers for their work in debating moral issues over the centuries. But what we want to take from them in this chapter is not their "points of discussion" but their *schema of debate*. While the talking and arguing are going on there is an ethical *framework* which, if understood and appreciated, can assist every decision maker in understanding where those with whom he is communicating are coming from and where they are headed ethically.

If a group from a regulatory agency tells an executive they do not care what it costs to clean up the plant's emissions, it just has to be done, then it would help the executive to understand the value position taken by the regulators. The real issue here is the question of whether or not the "good" set forth by the regulators is rightfully embodied in the requirement itself—getting rid of all plant emissions is "good" in itself. The business managers probably have a "net consequential" concept of "good" which offsets "goods" and "bads" to arrive at an optimal net "good" position. They would permit emissions as part of the "bad" in their evaluation so long as this "bad" is offset with a "good" product and "good" profit. We will return to this later, but the positions implied above are fundamentally different, and *there is* a strategy of reconciliation.

Issues of the type just mentioned will ultimately be settled at the "feet of truth" or at the "base of power." Realistically, both are at work in our culture. Every power base has an ethic and is involved in our culture's ethical schizophrenic struggle. But an ethical base is absolutely necessary to any person, group, or organization if they are to justify and legitimize themselves. A great deal of confrontation between groups in our culture flows directly from their value differences. Any group that cannot establish its moral base of operations cannot stand long in a free society. Libertarianism, egalitarianism, utilitarianism, and Marxism (four prominent systems of distributive justice to be discussed in Chapter 9) all stand on a different ethical premise. Ethics is either the calming oil on the water of conflict or the grease on the tracks of conflict and rapid change.

ETHICAL   Value judgments of a moral nature are
ROUTES   *all* made in connection with our "being"
                               and "doing." This is our first and grossest
breakdown of moral judgments. We assign a moral sense of right-

ness or wrongness to people's intentions, dispositions, motives, and traits of character—their "being" as they are. Thinking and all its qualitative aspects are subject to moral analysis. We also ascribe a moral value to people's behavior, actions, and deeds—their "doing" what they do. All of our physcial activity and its consequences are included under this category.

So the ethical highway is initially just two routes. As we shall see shortly, however, these each fork and have the potential of becoming two more routes. It can be diagrammed as follows:

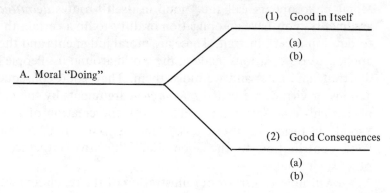

(1) Good in Itself

(a)
(b)

A. Moral "Doing"

(2) Good Consequences

(a)
(b)

The moral philosophers call these two branches the ethics of *moral obligation*—obligations, "oughts," and "shoulds" in deeds and acts—and the ethics of *moral value*—traits, motives, intentions, and character.

As stated, each of our two big branches is in turn divided into two paths. When you do something, the act is considered to be "good in itself" or to result in a "good consequence," if it is to be judged good. To illustrate, a "good in itself" act might be to encourage all of the employees of a firm to personally support the fund drive to enlarge the non-profit charitable children's hosptial. And a "results in good consequences" act might be to plow more profits back into product research and develop a new and better product that would cost less.

In the same manner, the idea of people being moral in their character and traits is divided into two categories—the virtue has value in itself or the virtue leads to a good consequence. As an illustration, "It is good to be honest" could be considered to have value in itself. Or, "Being honest keeps one out of jail" would be considered a good consequence of a good trait. Our diagram would now look like:

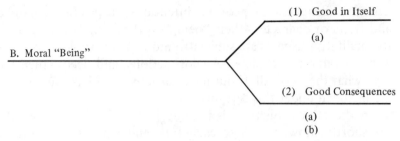

These are the two main routes and four subroutes of ethics. Moral philosophers call the "good in itself" routes *deontological* arguments—you have an obligation or duty to do a certain thing or to develop a certain trait. These are moral judgments and they are applied to observations made in the world around us. People judge us (traits and acts) and we judge them. The "good consequence" actions or virtues are called *teleological* arguments by the philosophers. This concept concerns itself with the creation of the most "good" in terms of "usefulness," "means to an end," or "make a good contribution to the good life," "positive influence," and other such results.

We will now return to our illustration of the regulators wanting all impure emissions eliminated from the plant. The regulators perceive that the elimination of such emissions is "good in itself." The business believes that producing its product is "resulting in a good consequence." The two parties are on two different highways. How do we bring them to a point of reconciliation?

There is no guarantee of reconciliation but there is no hope of it unless we can get both parties on the same "ethical highway." It is the effort to get all parties on the same ethical highway that helps us discover the alternatives of compromise or conflict. If, however, something is "true," "right," and "good" it can be carried along on either ethical branch of a main highway—"good in itself" or "good consequence" road. Moral "doing" that is "good in itself" will have a consequence and it *should* be "good" on balance. If this is not true, then we have discovered a real problems in our very perception of what is "good." Such inner conflicts are, unfortunately, all too present in our lives. As an example, if a manager holds that being honest is an absolute ethical "good in itself," but that being honest in this particular circumstance will probably prevent him from consummating an important sale, he is faced with an internal ethical conflict. He has a conflict between being honest—ethically "good in itself"—and making the sale—the act produces a "good consequence." The physical sale is a nonmoral ethical good (this concept will be covered in detail in the very next section of this chapter) but the *means* to achieve it—withholding information or telling a lie—are not ethically neutral. Suddenly, we are in conflict and face a temptation. But let us return once again to the regulators and their concerns with our plant emissions.

The business managers need to admit to themselves, and to the regulators, that the elimination of all impure emissions is "good in itself." That would be nice. We would all enjoy that. Then there needs to be an admission that the action necessary to accomplish this will produce a "consequence"—closing the plant or setting higher prices for the product. The regulator needs to admit this. The question now is, when does the consequence of one decision outweigh the consequence of another action? In this way we soon get to the real problems. How clean is clean air; what is an acceptable level of pollution; and what consequences are manifested in the face of each alternative? These are the hard, but real, questions in this case. Arguing that each other's values are right or wrong will not help solve a problem. Identifying the real problem is essential, and identifying the ethical highway one is traveling on helps greatly in clarifying the differences.

What our culture has not resolved is who is to have the responsibility for saying what is "good." There is a power struggle underway and the opposing forces ebb and flow. Who do we trust to have the wisdom to balance and harmonize the tensions that can and do exist between and within the complexities of doing what is "good in itself" and doing what has "good consequences"? Where is there such wisdom? Business wants the right to decide. Does their behavior warrant our trust? Government leaders claim they must be the arbiters. Upon what grounds do we presume they are so enlightened as to have the necessary wisdom? The intellectual community often points to itself as the potential "saviour." Have they shown that they can relate "facts" and "values"?

The ethics of "doing" is the exposed ethic. The ethic of "being" is the hidden ethic. It is falsely believed by too many that the ethic of "doing" is the public, business, and government ethic while the ethic of "being" is the private and personal ethic. This is a false dichotomy. This erroneous perception flows from the assumption that the competitive market place will force people to *do* what is good for others and therefore the decision makers' personal motives, intentions, and character traits are of no importance in the public arena. When acting publicly they are assumed to be guided by their rational faculties. When there was a broad cultural consensus about what was right and wrong that undergirded the culture's rational processes, this idea had some apparent validity, but in an ethically schizophrenic society this does not hold to be true. Why? When a culture accepts that there is no ethical consensus, the door is thrown wide open for tolerating, winking at, excusing, and/or accepting a wide variety of orientations within an assumed rational mind set. *What is rational is to a considerable degree shaped by what is believed to be ethical.*

Our attitudinal virtues are carried directly into our business activities. This shapes both our decisions and how we treat one another. There is a big difference between seeing people as a means to the end of profit making or in understanding profits to be a reflection of our having served people well. An attitude of being committed to doing what is right will obviously affect our business conduct, and this will in turn affect our sales, profits, and prices too over the long-run. It is just very naive to assume that the ethics of "being" is not closely tied to, and deeply influencing, our ethics of "doing."

RULES AND   How do people decide whether or not an
VIRTUES IN ETHICS   "act" is good in itself or results in a good
                          consequence? What is the standard or
criteria by which this is decided? Generally speaking, people either look to some form of "rule" for making such judgments or rely upon a personal, flexible criteria. This can be diagrammed for the ethics of moral "doing" as follows:

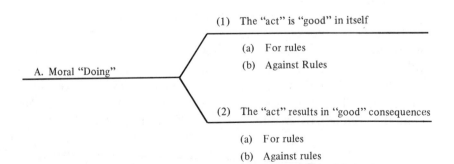

(1) The "act" is "good" in itself

A. Moral "Doing"

    (a) For rules
    (b) Against Rules

(2) The "act" results in "good" consequences

    (a) For rules
    (b) Against rules

When someone says an act is good in itself—eliminate all emissions from a factory—he or she is basing this value on some standard (rule) developed from natural observation or received from an authority as a statement of truth or fact. Or the judgment is based on the particular situation, personal feeling, intuition, or the prevailing practice at the time. These concepts of determining right are developed in the manner described in Chapters 4-6 and are used to support the set of ethics described in Chapters 2-3.

The dominant business ethic in our culture takes the form of utilitarianism—creating the most "net good" on balance. Businesses typically use an input-output analysis, cost benefit analysis, or formulate a generally conceived concept of what is a net good consequence. Most decision makers feel better when decisions are reduced to some measurable form—costs, revenues, and profits. From this general framework came the idea that the decisions generating the most profits were the best ones. But culturally we have begun to move from profit maximization, toward profit optimization, and on to the socialization of profits. Our public concern has to a considerable degree centered on wealth redistribution for about fifty years. So value conflicts arise over what is a just distribution of our wealth.

Then there are those who deem an act to be "good in its consequences" when it gives them a perception that they are personally better off mentally and/or physically than they were before the event occurred. This is psychological or ethical egoism. Generally, this act is viewed as being good for this time and circumstance but is not to be viewed as a norm.

So we have those who like rules, standards, and guides and we have those who look to themselves or situations to make their judgments. They all want the most of what they perceive to be "good."

Next we will look at the ethics of moral "being." Again the questions need to be answered: How do people decide if a motive, intention, disposition, or character virtue is good in itself or has a good consequence? What virtues are good? Here people make judgments based upon their identity and assessment of traits and virtues. This can be diagrammed as follows:

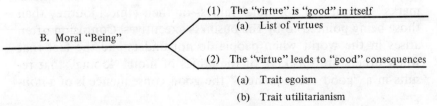

B. Moral "Being"

(1) The "virtue" is "good" in itself

    (a) List of virtues

(2) The "virtue" leads to "good" consequences

    (a) Trait egoism

    (b) Trait utilitarianism

Moral virtues may be assessed in the same way we assess moral acts. People generally assume our moral virtues are alterable and that certain human traits ought to be cultivated in people. There is a "division of the house," however, on how such virtues are to be brought about within the life of a person. Some look to parental training; others look to education; some speak of predisposition; others look to conversion experiences; some talk of determinism; others say it is a combination of all the aforementioned items; and all have their ideas without the power or ability to persuade the others. But all agree that virtues are extremely important.

For some, like the orthodox Christians, the intentions, motives, and virtues are the *most* basic building blocks of ethics. They perceive that when one's "being" is "good" or healthy, then the person's actions will automatically flow from the good root. Others with high commitments to the moral position see character traits as very important, too, but do not put the same emphasis on them. For two dimensional humanists, "good acts" are the key to understanding if people are virtuous. Their underlying motives are of little concern. So the "good man" is defined differently by different groups—some by acts alone and others by motives and acts.

In business ethics, however, we rarely hear or read of the importance of moral values as they pertain to our "being a person"; or of their importance as the wellspring of our actions. Business ethics is generally limited to the ethics of moral "doing." But an individual who is committed to being ethical should examine both ethical highways when making decisions. There are certainly differences of opinion about what is moral. But there are some broad consensuses in certain areas on what is immoral, and immorality is grounded in the traits, motives, intentions, and dispositions of people. No one disagrees that over the long haul our acts reflect our thoughts and motives.

MORAL AND NONMORAL VALUES   In the opening paragraph of this chapter it was noted that ethical backseat drivers can be looking for different "landmarks"—moral and nonmoral values—on their ethical journey than those being pointed to by the business executives. Confusion often arises in the world when people do not understand the fact that when others are speaking of the ethics of moral "doing" that results in a "good consequence," the good consequence is of a *non-*

moral quality. Or, put differently, we are assumed to have a moral obligation to act in a way that will result in the creation of the most good, nonmoral consequences—quality of products, level of profits, etc.

This moral obligation to create nonmoral consequences produces both a haven and a blindspot for decision makers. The haven is found in the fact that it seems safer to spend our time focused on nonmoral "things": products, services, jobs, profits, and a host of other nonmoral "ends." And the market place defines their goodness by purchasing or rejecting them. And we humans are being moral by simply involving ourselves in the process. This focus often causes other moral considerations to be assumed or to fade into the background. Problems of whether the "most good" is to be shared by the most people or if the distribution can be lopsided and still be just is not directly addressed by our system. Our earlier discussion on equality and inequality is once again important to recall here (pages 52-55).

A blindspot is also often created by separating nonmoral acts from moral values. This is where many have been led astray and believe that business ethics and personal ethics are different. What we do in business is often viewed as being "in the business" and "for the business." And all of this has its purpose in creating nonmoral goods. We can be viewed as agents of the business and our personal code of ethics is to be left at home, for our responsibility is to do what is best for the business—a nonmoral "being" under the law, producing nonmoral products and services. For some, humans (moral "beings") working for a nonmoral legal entity are to assume the role of being rational *nonmoral* decision makers whose job is to optimize nonmoral goals for the corporation. Some people rationalize in the face of this dehumanizing view—we are nonmoral decision makers—that it is acceptable to ignore personal moral principles when it is done for the nonmoral corporation (in its name) and helps in creating more nonmoral goods, services, market share, or profits. (Example: "I do not steal in my personal life, but I would pay to get a copy of my competitor's detailed plans.") These people believe that obtaining nonmoral "ends"—profits, market share, etc.—does not necessitate the maintenance of strict moral "means." Or, all is fair in love (business) and war.

The "fly in the ointment" is discovered in the dichotomy that is created between the humans who are deemed to be morally responsible individuals and the business which is considered by law, and by many individuals, to be a nonmoral entity that can be neither moral or immoral. A moral being—human—cannot serve a man-created nonmoral institution—business—and be moral without assuming the responsibility for *all* moral matters, whether they flow from human traits and actions or from the consequences of dealing with nonmoral "goods" which impact humans. The impact of nonmoral "goods" creates many side moral consequences. People are moral beings performing moral acts. Therefore, moral people cannot be allowed to create a nonmoral entity—business—and thereby act as if they serve a higher, nonmoral "being" that is immune to moral considerations. Theologically, this is idolatry—serving and worshipping the created. Philosophically, it is foolish because the business does nothing that is not humanly directed and related. Practically, it is folly because those affected by it will ultimately sweep the false mask aside if those behind it do not act ethically and cause the created entity to serve responsibly. To do otherwise is to pretend that right and wrong are inconsequential.

GROUNDS FOR GOOD The next question that must be faced is, on what basis does anyone declare that any act or trait is "good"? Philosophers call this the question of *intrinsic worth.* If we say an act is good in itself we must be able to say on what basis we declare it to be good. Stopping the impure emissions from our imaginary factory might be declared to be good by the regulators on the grounds that it will contribute to better *physical health,* which is an intrinsic good.

Intrinsic good may be ascribed to physical, mental, and spiritual categories, and there are a host of possible specific breakdowns under each. Hedonism—the balance of pleasure over pain—is a widely accepted good. Then, of course, there are debates over whether we are talking about the quantity of pleasure or the quality of it. Others see power as the baseline good and perceive almost everything as relating to it. Some would speak of truth or excellence or happiness or peace as the great intrinsic good. Others see all of these as constituting what is good. The Orthodox Christians see all created things as being intrinsically good because God created them and declared them to be good. This is the broadest concept of "good." But everyone has his standard for "good."

Decision makers need to identify their basis for believing that something is good. This is the last important link in the ethical chain before coming to the "padlock of ethics"—how do we *justify* our normative ethical judgments? And if our padlock does not hold the chain around our ethical system, it will in all probability be swept away in a storm of challenge. (Chapter 8 surveys the available "ethical padlocks.")

SUMMARY

We have identified the ethical routes people follow and the rules and virtues they use to decide which acts or virtues are good in themselves and which ones have good consequences. People get on these routes by virtue of being human—they are "beings" who "act."

Our conclusions about which standards (rules) to use, if any, and which virtues are most important are formed as we live life. Through the use of our reason, empirical experiences, existential and spiritual experiences, and personal interpretative conclusions—described in Chapters 4-6—we make our own judgments about what is morally right and wrong. Our values are formed and tested. We change, grow, become rigid, gain tolerance, or form other personal characteristics. We decide what is good and proceed to act upon it. In living it out, we declare our general ethic—two broad ethics were described in Chapters 2-3—and take positions in life.

ETHICAL ROUTES, RULES, AND VIRTUES

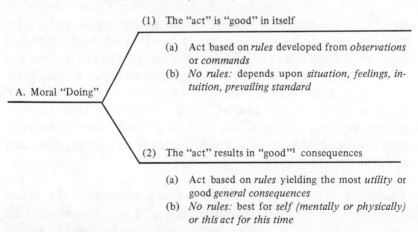

(1) The "act" is "good" in itself

    (a) Act based on *rules* developed from *observations* or *commands*

    (b) *No rules:* depends upon *situation, feelings, intuition, prevailing standard*

A. Moral "Doing"

(2) The "act" results in "good"[1] consequences

    (a) Act based on *rules* yielding the most *utility* or good *general consequences*

    (b) *No rules:* best for *self (mentally or physically) or this act for this time*

[1] This good is a nonmoral good resulting from performing a moral obligation to act and do something.

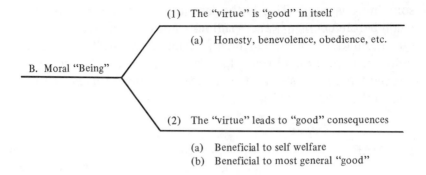

(1) The "virtue" is "good" in itself

     (a) Honesty, benevolence, obedience, etc.

B. Moral "Being"

(2) The "virtue" leads to "good" consequences

     (a) Beneficial to self welfare
     (b) Beneficial to most general "good"

Four illustrations of people's ethical routes will be given now as a practice in identifying where people are coming from and where they are going ethically. In life we should gather converging evidence over a period of time before concluding that someone habitually operates from a particular point of view. But listening carefully will almost always reveal where someone is ethically on a particular subject at that particular point in time. Identifying ethical routes is important for purposes of understanding, clarification, and moving to get discussants on the same ethical track where reconciliation becomes a possibility.

Illustration 1   A plant manager is speaking to a maintenance supervisor—"Jim, when we shut assembly line number 3 down next week to replace the conveyor system, I want you to make sure we get that line back in operation within 12 days. Every day after that costs us $100,000 more, so see if you can get the electricians and mechanics to cooperate and not be so legalistic about staying within the bounds of their defined work agreement. The union has tied us up so badly. A mechanic will hardly pull a wire from one side of the conveyor to the other, to help an electrician, if the crew boss is around. It is so silly and just cost us all money, time, and aggravation."

Analysis 1   Our speaker is dealing with the ethics of moral "doing" and is concerned with the "acts" resulting in "good" consequences. In this instance, the speaker is not in favor of the "rules" and desires a change for "this act for this time." (See the outline on page 121 for comparison.) The concern is for the nonmoral "good" of cost reduction ($100,000 per day). We do not know the basis for considering this "end" good or how the position would be justified if required.

The major ethical highway and the alternate subroute (good in itself or good in its consequences) are generally revealed in a conversation. The desire to follow or abandon rules is frequently revealed but may need to be determined. Whether one is focused on a moral and/or nonmoral good is generally clear. The basis—pleasure, power, love, excellence, etc.—for considering the "end" to be good is most often masked and will only be found with questioning. And rarely is the process of how one justifies a position given without asking for it. This tends to make people very defensive because the question approaches their last line of defense.

Illustration 2   A marketing vice president is speaking to an advertising executive—"Look, Bob, I don't care if the statistics do show that this kind of ad has good pulling power or not. To me, it offends the limits of good taste by appealing to the baser side of human nature. You are just going to have to come up with a different approach."

Analysis 2   Our speaker is rejecting a particular ethic of moral "doing" that would probably result in a good consequence—the ad will have good pulling power—from the posture of perceiving it to be in bad taste by appealing to the "less than virtuous" or less than best aspects of people's nature. By inference, the speaker will only accept the ethic of moral "doing" which results in a good consequence when it is compatible with the speaker's view of a positive influence associated with a trait in the realm of the ethics of moral "being." No standard, rule, or virtue is given, if one is in mind. Neither do we know the basis for considering this "end" good or how the speaker would justify the decision. The advertising executive would be well advised to get an answer to some of these unknowns before he goes to work on the ad again, however.

Illustration 3   A president is speaking to two vice presidents—"Hank . . .George . . .I appreciate your coming in. I wanted to let you know before the rumors got flying that I finally concluded I had to release Ralph, and did so last night around 7 p.m. Even though he has been with our team as long as we have, his philosophy was getting further and further out of phase with what we just have to do. I am not looking for "yes" men, and he is technically competent, but he was pushing us more and more to take actions that simply are not "right." You remember last month when I called him down publicly—which I hate to do, it violates a person's dignity—for suggesting before the Board that we might get by with relaxing our safety standards in the mines and raising our net income with the dollars saved. After my public rebuke I told him in private how I hated to do that, but also told him that this kind of thinking was simply unacceptable. Lives and profits are not discussible as if they are part of the same category. Well anyway, three days ago he suggested to me, in private, another idea for helping our profits and it was just as far out of bounds ethically as was his safety reduction idea. The evidence has been converging for some time now that there is just a basic flaw in his values somewhere. I was afraid he would end up hurting everyone and he simply did not agree . . . He will receive nine months severance pay and will be allowed to exercise his stock options which he was already entitled to, but as of this morning he is out for good. I am sorry to have to share this sad news with you two. . . ."

Analysis 3   In this case the president is addressing the situation on the level of the ethics of moral "being." He sees Ralph as having intentions and values that will lead to negative consequences that will prove to be disadvantageous to the general good of all in the organization. The president is dealing with a moral value before it has a chance to be translated into a moral act with a bad consequence in the nonmoral arena, which in turn could physically harm people. The president's basis of "good" is partially revealed in his expressed concern for people's physical well being but his process of justifying his action is not set forth. A commitment to right is revealed but not its underpinnings.

Illustration   A foreman is speaking to a line worker—
4   "Morning, Henry. How's it going? Good!
                        I don't mean to be fussy, Henry, but you
have got to get that ring off your hand and in your pocket. You

know the rules. No rings around the machine . . . if you lost that hand it would mess up your fishing! Ha! Thanks! How are the kids doing? . . ."

Analysis 4   The foreman in this case is acting on the basis of the ethics of moral "doing" for the purpose of accomplishing a good consequence based on the acceptance of the appropriateness of the company's rules. His basis of "good" is grounded in the idea that it is good not to get physically hurt. He is also taking a moral action to prevent a nonmoral adverse consequence. How he would justify it is not explicitly explained. In fact, none of our four illustrations demonstrate the individual's final line of defense. And this is typical. (This will be demonstrated in the next chapter.)

Making value judgments leaves the decision maker very vulnerable in today's society. Our cultural presuppositions are no longer fairly homogeneous. And people are not as adverse to demanding an explanation for our actions now as they once were. So any of us can find our ethical backs up against the wall of accountability with little notice or preparation. The challengers will call for us to *justify* our ethical routes, rules, virtues, moral and nonmoral values, and basis for standing where we do. So how do we *justify* our normative ethical judgments?

BIBLIOGRAPHY

Brandt, R. B., *Ethical Theory.* Englewood Cliffs, New Jersey: Prentice-Hall, Inc., 1959.

Frankena, William K., *Ethics,* second edition. Englewood Cliffs, New Jersey: Prentice-Hall, Inc., 1973, 1963.

Jones, W. T.; Frederick Sontag; M. O. Beckner; and R. J. Fogelin, eds., *Approaches to Ethics,* second edition. New York: McGraw-Hill, Inc., 1969.

Melden, A. I., ed. *Ethical Theories,* second edition, with revisions. Englewood Cliffs, New Jersey: Prentice-Hall, Inc., 1967.

Pahel, Kenneth; and Marvin Schiller, eds., *Readings in Contemporary Ethical Theory.* Englewood Cliffs, New Jersey: Prentice-Hall, Inc., 1970.

Sellars, W. S.; and John Hospers, eds., *Readings in Ethical Theories,* second edition. New York: Appleton-Century-Crofts, Inc., 1970.

CHAPTER
EIGHT

LAST LINE OF DEFENSE: JUSTIFYING OUR ETHICS

INTELLECTUAL NAKEDNESS

Attempting to justify an ethical position that is held with deep conviction can be an unsettling experience. When we are among friends we enjoy stating our position on matters that are ethical in character—"They ought to lock him up and throw away the key." Friends rarely challenge us and call upon us to justify our posture. They reinforce us. There are some individuals who even enjoy a good rigorous debate when confronted by people who hold different values. But that is generally only true when conflicting positions are being presented and no' one is asking us to *justify* our view.

We generally become uncomfortable and defensive, however, when someone who differs with us persistently challenges us with a "Why do you believe that?" type of question. When this kind of question is repeated in the face of every answer, the uneasiness mounts rapidly. This kind of probing quickly strips us and exposes our understanding of *purpose* and *meaning.* Quickly we know we have little cover left behind which to hide. We are at the bottom of our well of understanding. We are exposed. We are intellectually

naked. Only the strength of our "true truth" is left. Is that sufficient? Or, will we be thought less of or even worse, ridiculed?

Most of us have learned somewhere in life that this kind of deep
and open exposure can leave us wounded and struggling to maintain
our own sense of dignity. This is particularly true if the probers
are still secure behind their unexposed defenses. Our instincts tell
us to be cautious and not to expose our last line of defense. This
is particularly the case when we are uncertain about our own basis
of justification. And if we are not sure of our own position, we
have little hope of convincing others. The reasons for feeling in-
secure are numerous. So people who are caught in such an uncomfortable position will often try to defensively deflect the "why"
questions thrust at them by turning them back on the original
questioner. Or, defensive (and defenseless) statements such as,
"That is just the way it is" are heard. That is a "close out" answer
that says, "I will not expose myself to you any further." Sometimes so much emotion is generated that displays of temper are
seen. But whatever the reaction, people will rarely voluntarily expose their last line of defense, unless they are very secure or are
absolutely forced to.

What is the last line of defense for all ethical justifications? The
bottom of the well is located in either the *natural* grounds of reality
or a *divine* base. When people point to their: (a) view of, (b) encounter with, or (c) historical evidence related to, (1) human nature,
(2) human conduct, or (3) the physical universe around them,
they are grounding their ethical judgments in the "natural order of
things." This is their last and deepest appeal. There are five positions of this type outlined on page 164 which, in itself, reflects the
wide diversity of approaches that exist within the body of those
appealing to the "natural order of things."

The divine base of justification is used by those who perceive a
divine reality undergirding the natural order of things and who see
this as giving specific meaning and purpose to their qualitative
judgments. Those who rely upon the divine premise may also appeal to the "natural order" as secondary and supporting evidence.
And their interpretations of human nature, their analysis of history,
and their qualitative perceptions of the physical universe are not
all alike either. This is reflected in the fact that there are seven of
these "divine" groups, arranged in four categories, that are outlined
in Table 8.1.

Table 8.1 Natural Base of Ethical Justification

A. Rational Primacy:
   The justification of an ethical position through the use of reason and logic as the primary means of interpreting the natural order.
   (B and/or C may be used secondarily.)

B. Empirical Primacy:
   The justification of an ethical position through the use of sensory observations as the primary means of interpreting the natural order.
   (A and/or C may be used secondarily.)

C. Existential/Intuitive Primacy:
   The justification of an ethical position through the use of one's experienced existence in relationship to the natural order through the use of feelings and/or intuition.

D. Ethical Agnosticism:
   The assertion that ethical certainty is unobtainable; ethical positions differ from person to person; the many competing positions prove its obscurity; ethics is always relatively related to truth; people's differences show there is no "normative right or wrong."

E. Ethical Atheism:
   The assertion that there is no basis for making ethical judgments; ethics is only attitudes; humans only evaluate and recommend; we cannot know true truth.

NATURAL BASE OF ETHICAL JUSTIFICATION
Those who ground their ethical justification in the "natural order of things" make an appeal to a particular process by which true truth should be ascertained. Some believe the natural order is best understood when approached from a position of logic and reason—rationalism. There are those who perceive that logic may prove to be illogical and that empirical observation is the best approach from which to draw conclusions—empiricism. Others rebel against both approaches and insist on the use of the existential and intuitive forms of determining the truth about the natural order. And finally, there are those who conclude, after using a process for some time, that ethics is either uncertain at best, or nonexistent in reality. These are all applied to the areas of assessing the nature of people, the interpretation of human conduct and the evaluation of the physical universe.

The process of ordering our perceptions—rational, empirical, etc.—does not provide a uniform concept of human nature or interpretation of human conduct either within or between the processing groups. Sometimes, in fact, their views are downright contradictory. Their view of man's responsibilities, rights, and concepts of fairness, justice, and appropriate benevolence vary tremendously. This is true even when we observe and address the same characteristics, traits, and actions. Some see humans as basically good. Others see them as basically evil. And there are those who see people as individuals who experience internal conflict with the pulls of good and evil. Others do not think in any of these categories.

Then there are other categories of analysis that are applied to studies of human nature. Many people believe that all human thoughts and actions are predetermined by genetics and that mankind is living fatalistically. A still larger group hold to some form of human determinism in which they see people making choices based on prior events and experiences. Choices are thus determined, according to this view, by the past. Others hold to a concept of influence which holds that all past events may be overridden by human choice, even if many are not, for good and sufficient reasons. Prior events do influence choices but are not determining them. And finally, many hold that man is an autonomous being with a free will to do as he chooses.

How we treat one another in our daily lives strongly reflects what we perceive to be the true nature of our species. For some, it is a "dog eat dog" world of social Darwinism—the strong and fit survive. For others, kindness is a necessary ingredient even when a hard and disruptive decision is reached—fire an individual or relocate a plant. Some have empathy and others do not care. For one, the situation is sad, and for the other, it reflects tough luck. We find people who are polite to those above them and rude to those beneath. There are those who trust people and those who trust no one. The differences are wide and astounding. Both what we decide to do and how we carry out our decisions reveal our ethical viewpoint.

The basic objective of decisions in business is often utilitarian in nature—produce the most net good benefits of a nonmoral quality—which flows from the moral obligation to create a good consequence. Often our real ethical sensitivity is revealed in how we *carry out* the utility-oriented decision. Here the quality of the goodness of the actions—implementing ones—and the traits of character—moral "being"—are exhibited as necessarily related parts of the decision that has a utilitarian objective. A nonmoral objective (produce a better product) can stand alone as producing a nonmoral consequence in our *minds* before any action is taken to implement it. But as soon as any action is taken, it is fraught with moral considerations and consequences. Because this perspective is so frequently lost, people often perceive the decision makers are more interested in "things" than people. And if so perceived, those adversely affected hold the decision makers to be unethical.

How we treat one another reflects rather accurately what we perceive to be the true nature of mankind. What we hold to have greatest value and believe is most important is carried directly into our decision making process. This has led many "natural order" based decision makers to conclude that how they would like to be treated is how they should treat others. This is known as "Golden Rule" ethics. Anything less than this is deemed by such people to be unethical and therefore hold it as an operating principle. (There are those who deny the validity of this principle on the grounds that individuals differ in their preference for personal treatment. Each reader should consider if such differences are general enough to invalidate the principle or would those who reject it be deviants from normal expectations.)

Decisions that are justified on the basis of the "natural order of things" reflect those traits, motives, characteristics, and actions which are deemed by the decision makers to be in keeping with their view of reality (truth). The process of deciding what is "true truth" was the basis of Chapters 4-6. They perceive that "this"— their trait or action—is "right" because it reflects accurately "truths" discerned from the natural order of things. As an illustration, a manager may perceive, based on his natural observation, that workers (presupposes *hard workers*) perform more productively in an environment where their personal efforts are recognized and rewarded than when everyone in the group is treated alike. So this manager builds in incentive systems to encourage individual effort. Yet another manager across town observes that too much individuality can lead to "competitive strain" which results in long-term problems for workers (assumes *average workers*). So he is more inclined to move toward a group solution than an individual one. He gives elaborate tests to the prospective employees to try and find people who are team oriented in their outlook. So two managers, both looking at the same world, but focusing on different characteristics, can and do draw different conclusions. The natural order is diverse and does not produce uniform approaches to reality or similar conclusions.

Major decisions, like relocating a plant, touch a myriad of ethical nerves. The corporation has a moral obligation to create the best nonmoral consequences it can. Its function is to participate in the allocation of scarce resources in the most efficient manner possible, within the appropriate legal and moral bounds—the latter is our subject. Businesses are publicly sanctioned to operate in a private property framework in the belief that all parties receive the most benefits when this is done. All managers, whether in business, labor, or government, are responsible for both "what" is done and "how" it is done within their sphere of decision making. This dual concept of ethics—"what" and "how"—is extremely important because it puts our decisions and actions into a holistic perspective. Living ethics is the combination of what we do and how we do it in the same way as a living person is both a physical and mental being. "What" we decide reveals our goals. "How" the decision is to be implemented reveals the ethical sensitivity or "heart" of those responsible. (Sensitivity itself is construed by many to be an important moral trait. Hence, to be insensitive to others is unethical or immoral.) If the ethical traits of empathy and gentleness are absent when the ethical obligation necessitates a tough and disruptive decision, the feelings of those hurt can easily override the reasonableness of the basic decision. Most decisions create a string of other decisions and corresponding actions. And our traits of character are exhibited at every turn. Large and small economic decisions are large and small ethical decisions.

As discussed in Chapters 4-6, when the process of determining truth was altered—the Hegelian dialectical synthesis began to replace the thesis-antithesis thinking—our culture began moving into its current state where it is experiencing severe ethical schizophrenia. If the demands for ethical "proof" become synomous with physical proof, as it has in the minds of many, our confidence in our ability to define and defend an ethical position erodes rapidly. For almost two generations universities in our culture have been developing the critical skill of challenging the "knowability" of all values. This has added tremendously to the subconscious desire to not have our ethical base or justification process openly challenged. The side effects of this have been an enlargement of the number of people who subscribe to the positions of the "ethical agnostic" and "ethical atheists"—see page 129 for the definition of each. This produces one of two consequences. Ethics either becomes the position of the individual or its possibility is denied altogether. In the face of our culture's growing economic interdependency where more cooperation and good will are required, our ethical fracturing appears to be out of step. Nevertheless, ethical agnosticism is attracting an increasing number of people who justify their ethics by denying the validity of any base. If the agnostic position is accepted as "true truth" and becomes the norm, our "right" and "wrong" *issues will, in the final analysis, need to be settled at the seat of power and not at the seat of truth.* Ethical schizophrenia draws us in that direction.

DIVINE BASE OF ETHICAL JUSTIFICATION Those who look to a divine grounding for their ethical justifications often feel even more vulnerable in their appeal for understanding than those who point to the natural order. They are more vulnerable in the sense that they are basing their view on a perceived reality that lies behind the tangible and observable reality of the natural order. When properly understood, however, several of our divine based groups are no more vulnerable to the modern day demands for "proof" than those who make a direct appeal to the "natural order"—Deists, Hindus, and Buddhists are in such a position. Those who subscribe to the view of a nonpersonal God— Deists—do so based upon natural revelation. The natural order of things is their "evidence." Their explanation is grounded in either the primacy of the rational, empirical, or existential/intuitive interpretations of reality or a combination of them. So one who appeals to the natural order of things as a justification base and those who rely upon a deistic perception of God both rest their case upon their perception of the natural order. Their appeals are to two different interpretative bases—a deistic God and the natural order— but by definition the deistic God offers no direct help to humans, apart from the natural order. So in this case we have differences in human perceptions that are not based upon external differences that are knowable or experienceable but are differences that are *internal,* personal, interpretative, and perceptual in character.

Pantheists—Hindus and Buddhists—while seeing things as a mode of the divine, do not ascribe a personal, communicative, relational (two independents relating to each other) quality to the divine. Their appeal is not to the tangible natural order either, however. The natural order appealed to by the deists is the external physical universe and the human conduct related to it. The natural order appealed to by the Hindus and Buddhists is that which is locked up deep within the "being." They teach that enlightenment comes through "working" at withdrawal from the world and entering into a contemplative time of meditation. It is not a contemplation of the world but a contemplation of the greater realities and truths that rest behind and within the illusory forms of physical reality.[1] Once again, human perceptions are seen to differ but such differences are not ascribed to external, knowable, or experienceable realities. The pantheists appeal to the natural order of an internal, personal, perceptual quality. The data appealed to by the pantheist and the deist are radically different. One's data is external and subject to observation. The other's is internal and subject to reflection. One is extroverted in character and the other introverted. But both appeal to that which is described as "obtainable by man's own effort." Neither appeal to special messages from the divine. The places they go to look are very different, but both are "natural" and available to all by their own searching and exercise of their volitional will.

The base of justification that is radically different from the "natural" based types and the divine based groups already discussed is the kind of justification that appeals to having contact and/or special messages from the divine. There are two major groups in this category and they are very different in character. There are those who speak of a "contact" experience without accompanying verbalized/action experiences and there are those who believe in "contact" experiences with verbalized/action content.

Those who speak of a "contact" experience without accompanying verbalized/action experiences are the "divine mystics." In our culture, the theological existentialists comprise the majority of those who fall into this category. These are the people who espouse a belief in the divine, based upon personal experience of a quality that persuaded them of both the reality and presence of the divine without, however, having any verbalized communication or observable physically related phenomenon occur in conjunction with the divine contact. Existential experiences may create varying intensities of feeling or intellectual acumen. The experiences are personal and nontransferable. They serve as a basis of hope in a gen-

---

[1] H. Saddhatissa, *Buddhist Ethics: Essence of Buddhism* (New York: George Braziller, Inc., 1970) pp. 33-85.

Table 8.2 Divine Base of Ethical Justification

A. God (Theism with degrees of personal involvement)
  1. Orthodox Jews justify ethics by:[1]
    1st: Special Revelation—Bible: Old Testament
    2nd: Natural Revelation—Observe the nature of things
  2. Orthodox Christians justify ethics by:[1]
    1st: Special Revelation—Bible: Old and New Testament
    2nd: Natural Revelation—Observe the nature of things
  3. Muslims justify ethics by:
    1st: Special Revelation—Koran and selected Bible segments
    2nd: Natural Revelation—Observe the nature of things

B. God (Deism with no personal involvement)
  1. Deists justify ethics by:
    a. Natural Revelation—Observe the nature of things and/or
    b. Existential Experience—Intuitive

C. Divine Pantheism (Nonpersonal in Character)
  1. Hindus justify ethics by:
    a. Intuition and meditation, and/or
    b. Natural Revelation—Observe the nature of things
  2. Buddhists justify ethics by:
    a. Intuition and meditation, and/or
    b. Natural Revelation—Observe the nature of things

D. Divine Mystical (Nondefinable in Character)
  1. Theological Existentialists justify ethics by:
    1st: Existential Experience—Intuitive mystical
    2nd: Natural Revelation—Observe the nature of things

[1] Those who perceive of themselves as conservative Jews or as neo-orthodox Christians may also perceive of God as defined in either category B or category D. Reformed Jews and liberal Christians appeal to the "natural order of things."

eral but not a specific sense. The general hope is in the perception of the reality of a divine force which holds out hope that there is meaning and purpose in life. Without a communicated message the benefits of the experience are limited to their impact on the experiencer. The nonexperiencers are left out, except to the extent of knowing that the other individual has had an existential experience.

Our second group, those who accept special revelation in the form of verbalized communications and divine activity in the time, space dimensions of the natural order, is comprised of the Jews, Christians, and Muslims who are of an orthodox persuasion. There are other individuals or even large groups who also attest to a belief in special revelation but our discussion will be limited to these three with their common heritage and roots in the Bible. The Mus-

lims accept the first five books of the Bible, the Psalms of David,
the *ethical* teaching of Matthew, Mark, Luke, and John.[2] They
reject the Gospel teachings about Jesus being God incarnate and
the only saviour of mankind. The Koran (Quran) is their primary
special revelation, but as descendants of Abraham, they claim the
above parts of the Bible as special revelation as well. The Koran is
the final authority, however, where differences occur.

The Jews who accept the Old Testament and the Christians who
understand the entire Bible to be special revelation see it as God's
revelation of himself and of his will for mankind. Just as one does
not rely upon a "leap of faith" to believe that his great grandfather
lived, whom he never knew, or to believe that there was an Alex-
ander the Great (356-323 B.C.), the orthodox Christians or believing Jews see no necessity for a "leap of faith" to believe in God as
the creator, sustainer, and saviour. For them, God has spoken;
God has acted; and it is recorded for all to read and examine in the
Bible. For the orthodox Christians, Jesus Christ is the reference
point for all ethical justifications. Who he was, what he did, and
what he said serves as the standard. For the Jews, God's command-
ments are the norm. For these, the Bible is an accurate historical
account of God's revelation of himself and, as such, is the normative record to be used in evaluating all personal actions, decisions,
experiences, situations, and attitudes. To violate its norm is to do
what is wrong.

**COMMON
GROUND**   While the differences between and within
our divine and natural based groups are
vast, there is a common ground in the
"natural order of things." While the *natural order* is the primary
source for some and only the secondary source for others, it *is
the only common point of reference around which all can converse.*
Those who subscribe to the natural base of ethical justification
differ in their interpretation and perceptions but not in their agreement that people must incorporate in some manner what is
physically outside them and mentally within them for determining
and justifying their position. Their emphases differ but the raw
materials are the same.

[2] David G. Bradley, *A Guide to the World's Religions* (New Jersey: Prentice-Hall, Inc.,
1963) p. 71.

Those who subscribe to the divine base of ethical justification really divide into those who believe in special communicative revelation and those who do not. Those who do not accept special revelation in a communicative form either join the naturalists—the deists join them; redefine the territory for exploring the natural— the Hindus and Buddhists subscribe to introspection rather than the external reality; or they incorporate their mystical experience into their interpretation of the natural order.

Those who accept special communicative revelation are separated from the other groups by the fact that they believe in an externally given standard for right and wrong. The "natural order" ethically based groups all believe that the human is individually responsible for determining the true standard. Does man determine the ethical standard or is the standard given to mankind by God? The answer to this question divides our world. And those who believe in special revelation are divided into three major groups: those who accept the Old Testament, but who still await the Messiah or the Messianic Era—Jews; those who accept the Old and New Testament as true truth—orthodox Christians; and those who accept only parts of the old and New Testament plus the Koran—the Muslims. These three have the same root but become very different trees with different fruit. They agree on the need for, and availability of, an external standard. They differ on what it is.

The closest we can come to having a common ground is in the use of the "natural order of things." As stated above, some use it as their primary point of reference and others as their secondary or supporting point of reference. So what do we do? We learn to identify our own grounds of justification and prepare to stand up and be counted. If we will not, others with whom we differ will rise and lead us where we do not want to go.

STAND UP AND BE COUNTED When people are pushed to justify their position, they need to identify their ethical base of justification in sufficient detail so that others can see the influence it has on the development and direction of their position. Then they should move to connect their personal ethical base with time, space, historic data related to the "natural order" that is under discussion in the practical arena of business. When a position is taken in the name of business, where many ethical bases may be represented, the composite results will need to be presented on the "common ground" level—the natural order of things—stating that what follows emerged as a consensus or as the majority position, whichever is the case. Then you lay out the full decision and are counted, with the knowledge that some will agree while others will not.

To illustrate this process we will assume that four vice presidents of a drug manufacturer have two opposing conclusions and four different bases of justification in the following situation. The research lab has just reported the discovery of a compound—called 483—that if taken orally, one capsule every thirty days, will cause a fertilized ovum to separate from the wall of the uterus around the twelfth day following conception and pass with no more complications that a routine menstruation. The drug produces a form of starvation that sets in around the second day following conception and completes the cessation function within eight to ten days with absolutely no side effects biologically. The drug can be economically produced so as to reduce the current cost of chemical birth control to one eighth its present cost.

We will assume that the four people had been stating their opinions and positions for some time when one of them suggested that they were all really avoiding the "bottom line" of their views, and that it would really help all of them if each would share his or her deepest base of justification. They each agreed to do this.

V-P 1—"You all may be my friends, but in light of what we have just agreed to do, I feel like a rooster on parade in front of three foxes. Be kind, my friends—here goes—I really believe we ought to produce the 483 compound. Nobody here debates its marketing and profitability potentials. They are enormous. The gutsy issue we are hung up on is the ethical implications of producing an abortive medication. I find nothing unethical about giving people this option. The intrauterine devices have been out now for years, and they accomplish the same end, but with more potential complications . . . but that is riding another horse and not defending my own. Well, I believe people have the right to make these kinds of choices in life. Their dignity demands they be given such choices. No one knows if the human has a soul or not, for sure . . . I believe that we do . . . but God gave us the responsibility to make such choices. When He wound this world up and set it in motion, I believe He left all ethical choices up to us to discover and live out. For me, love is the greatest operating principle. Why should someone have a child who does not want it? Where is the love in that? And besides, I just don't believe there is any meaningful life at two to twelve days following conception. If that is wrong, it is less wrong than having children and not wanting them."

Justification 1—The ethics of "doing," with a "good consequence" of generating high, nonmoral profits is accepted and not debated by any of the four. Is this to be overridden by other moral considerations? The ethics of "being" is appealed to here on the basis of supporting the "dignity" of people—"good in itself"—and fostering the virtue of "love"—a good trait in itself. This is all to avoid a bad consequence of "doing" which can end in having unwanted children. The *justification base* is grounded in a deistic belief in God as one who "wound this world up" and "left all ethical choices up to us"—no special revelation to help. Without divine help, man is free to, and responsible for, making the best choice possible. And there is an intuitive judgment that there is no "meaningful life at two to twelve days following conception."

V-P 2—"Bob, you and I really come out on this at different places. And I am fascinated, too, that a person who believes in the existence of God would arrive at a "produce" conclusion, while someone like me, who doesn't accept or reject a position about God, would conclude that it is wrong to produce such a compound. I have thought and thought about this whole issue of abortion and there are some logical and rational extensions of it that scare me to death—no pun intended. I end up seeing a bunch of Hitler's running around every time I think of it. Let me explain. If I hold a dried pea in my hand, it has a germ in it that can burst forth into fruitful life if given the proper environment. It has life in itself as it is . . . dried or flowering. So a fertilized egg, one second old, is life . . . developing human life. I think it is morally wrong to take human life. I don't want you taking mine . . . before birth, at birth, at age forty, at age eighty, or ever. And that is what really frightens me. It is just as logical for our society to allow mercy killings and genocide of the elderly for reasons that are rationalized on anything from "love" to economic necessity. Life is natural. Death is frightening. It is the End! Nobody wants it for themselves. Life is good. Our company would condone and economically benefit from abortion if we produce and market Compound 483 . . . it all sounds more like 'Camp 483' to me!"

Justification 2—This person presents herself as an agnostic—

"who doesn't accept or reject a position about God"—whose *justification base* is a combined rational/empirical approach to the "natural order of things"—"some logical and rational extensions," ". . . dried pea . . . it has a germ in it"; "just as logical for our society"; "life is natural." The ethics of "doing" (taking life) has a bad consequence (death is bad) and the ethics of "being" (having life) is good in itself (life is good). Life is a good value.

V-P 3—"Wow, Mary your logic is impeccable, I join you in your conclusion, even though my basis is quite different. Human life is valuable beyond measure, in my judgment. Bob, I too believe God put this universe in motion. But I don't think He just wound it up and left us to determine what is ethical. I believe God created the earth and has performed many acts over the centuries to reveal himself and help us, which are carefully recorded in the Bible. And I do believe humans have a soul, even though the Bible does state clearly that no man knows when the human spirit comes to the body being formed in the womb. So for me, decisions to abort life are playing God. And I don't want to have any connection with anything that takes human life since I believe Christ was God giving His life for me so I could have life . . . an abundant life now and eternal life later. I believe that one day I am going to stand before Christ and give an account of all my motives and actions and I don't want to do that, or encourage that, which is contrary to his character. And Bob, I really take exception to using "love" as a justification for chemical abortion. In my opinion, that is "self love" in disguise. That is certainly not the kind of love God exhibited or talked about in the Bible. I would like to see us take Compound 483 and do some more research to see if we could adapt it to use in pest and insect control. But I simply think it is wrong for us to promote this compound as a method of birth control."

Justification 3—This individual's *justification base* is that of the Orthodox Christian—the Bible is accepted as propositional truth from God. He accepts the Biblical account of creation; he believes God's acts or revelation are accurately recorded; he believes people are body and spirit (a unified soul); he understands God to love life; and he believes Jesus was God incarnate. This forms his base of reasoning. The ethics of moral "doing" is also appealed to on the basis of an ultimate consequence—"one day I am going to stand before Christ and give an account of all my motives and actions." His perceived basis of "good" is God and his love.

V-P 4—"All of you sound like you know what you believe. Well, I know that none of us *know* anything with certainty. We cannot be sure about our opinions . . . they differ from person to person. Your three different perceptions prove my point. I look out on the world and all I see are differences of opinion everywhere and on everything. We are a business, my friends . . . not a philosophy class or church. The product is a compound, not a "god." People will make their own choices. We are not going to decide for them. We are sitting here trying to make a decision for other autonomous people. No way can we do that. Its consequence for them is their business. For us, it means big profits. For the world, it means a cheap, safe method of birth control is available. The sheer weight of this alone says, 'Go!" The decision is a simple one, as far as I am concerned."

Justification 4—The discussion turns full circle to an appeal for the ethics of moral "doing" for two consequential reasons: there will be large profits and there will be a simple, cheap means of dealing with the world's population problems. This person has made a strong appeal to return the whole matter to the level of nonmoral values (products and profits) and let the world worry about the morality. His *justification base* is that of the "ethical agnostic"—you cannot know what is ethical with any degree of certainty. He asserts that everyone is offering opinions and perceptions, but not knowable facts. He holds this based on natural observation—their discussion.

What has occurred in the conversation between these four vice-presidents does not resolve the question—two want to make the compound and two don't—but it opens up the level of understanding. It clearly clarifies their presuppositions and should produce a deeper understanding of one another. The firm's president or board of directors will not receive a consensus recommendation on this production and marketing question.

We have identified many problems that make it virtually impossible for us culturally to establish an ethical consensus. How then does one "get a handle" on the larger social question, "What are the corporations' social responsibilities?"

BIBLIOGRAPHY

Bade, William Frederic, *The Old Testament in the Light of Today; A Study in Moral Development.* New York: Houghton Mifflin Company, 1915.

Barth, Karl, *Church Dogmatics.* Authorized translation by G. T. Thompson. New York: Scribner, 1955.

Descartes, Rene, *Discourse on the Method of Rightly Conducting the Reason and Seeking the Truth in the Sciences,* translated from the French and collated with the Latin by John Veitch. Chicago: The Open Court Publishing Company, 1935.

Kant, Immanuel, *Immanuel Kant's Critique of Pure Reason,* translated by Norman Kemp Smith. London: Macmillan and Co., Ltd., 1963.

Katy, Steven T., *Jewish Ideas and Concepts.* New York: Schochen Books, 1977.

Locke, John, *An Essay Concerning the Understanding, Knowledge, Opinion and Assent,* edited with an introduction by Benjamin Rand. Cambridge, Mass.: Harvard University Press, 1931.

Saddhatissa, H., *Buddhist Ethics: Essence of Buddhism.* New York: George Braziller, Inc., 1970.

Sartre, Jean Paul, *Exisentialism and Humanism,* translation and introduction by Philip Mairet (1st English edition). London: Metheun, 1940, 1970.

Schaeffer, Francis A., *The God Who Is There.* Downers Grove, Illinois: Inter-Varsity Press, 1968.

Torrey, Norman Lewis, *Voltaire and the English Deists.* New Haven: Yale University Press, 1930.

CHAPTER
NINE

BUSINESS SOCIAL RESPONSIBILITY

We have just discussed how four vice presidents of a drug manufacturer can have divergent views on the ethical questions associated with the production of an abortive compound. Businesses face myriads of such questions when dealing with issues such as product safety, employee safety, employment discrimination, ethics of advertising, appropriateness of government regulations, environmental protection, stockholder responsibility, conflicts of interest, and a host of other topics. How do business executives come to grips with these many areas of responsibility? The truth is that most respond to the questions only as they erupt in "corporate brush fires." Few executives have a system within which to examine, sort out, and resolve to their personal satisfaction such issues.

This chapter is designed to develop a conceptual framework that can be used to: (a) identify the fundamental issues; (b) help in understanding the true ethical differences and consequences that emanate from the selection of an ethical choice; and (c) encourage thoughtful commitment to an ethically coherent, consequential position. In doing this, three very broad areas of consideration will be examined dealing with: (1) personal values that are applied to

groups of people; (2) distributive justice; and (3) identifying who
is morally responsible for the corporation's social responsibility.
From these we will develop two disjoining principles—those that
force the separation of ethical positions—that, when applied to
the actual issues that confront us, will assist in cutting through
the bulk of the emotional and short-run pressures that accompany
most "hot" issues. Once the decision maker formulates his or her
"guides," their application will greatly reduce the tension and
facilitate communications with others by helping to identify
those points where honest differences occur in ethical judgments.

**PERSONAL VALUES
AND GROUPS**
The right and wrong of what people
think about and how they act with regard to themselves and one another is
the heart of ethics. Most people have a fairly well defined set of
normative judgments about their personal ethics. Opinions on
personal matters that concern stealing, lying, sex, crude language,
physical harm, and one's relationship to authority are basic to our
daily lives. Our thinking and behavior reflect our true commitment
(or its absence) to values associated with such subjects.

Our personal/interpersonal values serve as the foundation for all
of the larger, more complicated issues we face in life. So when
machinists, foremen, secretaries, salesmen, legal assistants, plant
managers, vice presidents, or chairmen of the board come to work,
they arrive with their personal code of ethics and this is what they
are going to interpret (reinterpret), apply, and live out in their daily
lives at work. Those who are "sloppy" in their personal values—
insensitive to issues of right and wrong or their behavior deviates
from their own normative concepts—will also be prone to exhibit
the same ethical conduct (standards) at work. The reverse is also
true. Those whose personal code of ethics is well defined and
deeply committed to will tend to maintain the same high standards
and commitment while at work. As we are personally, so we tend
to be at work. An important exception to this is discussed in the
following paragraph.

What does happen in the work environment, however, is that
decisions often prove to be far more complex and far-reaching in
their potential consequences. Another important dimension is also
present in a corporate setting that is not common to our personal

or social experiences. The decision maker in a business setting is serving as an agent or representative of the business. This can and does, on occasion, raise two more possibilities for conflict: (a) between the short-run professional interests of the representative and the long-run interests of the corporation—make our current operating profits look better by postponing certain maintenance work; and (b) by allowing one's service to the corporation—a nonmoral entity whose end is the creation of nonmoral goods and services—to become so pervasive that the decision maker rationalizes that he or she can assume the nonmoral character of the corporation and pretend that his or her decisions are nonmoral in quality (the corporation is doing "it"). This last condition is fraught with ethical pitfalls and many individuals find themselves in deep inner conflict because they try to pretend they are nonmoral agents. An impossible state for a human. (A review of the section, Moral and Nonmoral Values, in Chapter 8, might be helpful to the reader at this time.) These factors—rising complexity of decisions, expanded consequences, conflict between personal and corporate interests, and possible attempts to be nonmoral agents—all increase the pressure on decision makers but do not change their basic, normative, personal values.

Right and wrong are right and wrong in any context—personal decisions or business ones. Those who like to think of decisions as being "grey" in nature should not be "turned off" by the language of "right" and "wrong." There are times when making any choice, or not making one, will leave some people in an injured position. Nothing will alter this fact. Sometimes the only choice people have is to decide which group is to be helped and which is to be unaided or, on occasion, even injured. So once a decision is made, the "grey" aspect is effectively treated as if it no longer existed. By action or inaction a position is declared to be the correct one.

An example of the above would be a company's adoption of an employment policy that incorporated the principles of "affirmative action." When such a policy is adopted, the consequences will produce the side effect of reverse discrimination. This means the historic majority is now going to be discriminated against in certain cases, causing injury. On the other hand, if a policy of "nondiscrimination" is adopted, those who have been injured by previous acts of discrimination and thereby left in an underdeveloped condition—health, education, cultural, economic, social—will not receive compensatory justice or a helping hand in overcoming the disadvantages that accrued to them under the former conditions of injustice. Consequentially they are left with their disadvantages and the new policy of nondiscrimination merely says that the past harmful practices will now stop. Either choice—affirmative action or nondiscrimination—can and will be called unjust by those who disagree with the adopted policy. Life presents us with a lot of such issues and choices. Call them "grey" but once choices are made there has been a declaration by those who made it that choice "x" is the "right" one.

Let us once again return to the thesis that it is our personal ethics that we bring to group or corporate decisions and that there is no separate "business ethics" apart from the application of our personal ethics—ethics related to lying, stealing, etc. To highlight this we will look at a few illustrations that concern themselves with several aspects and types of stealing found in the personal and business arenas.

Most people would normatively agree that it is unethical for one person to steal from another one. Such behavior is widely perceived to be destructive within the social fabric. But our level of *commitment* to or *tolerance* allowed from such a normative concept can and does vary a great deal. We will begin by examining the "easy" area of stealing—the taking of money and goods.

If someone steals an automobile, alters its serial number, and then resells it, we generally consider the act to be a criminal one. If three men abscond with twelve cows from your farm at night, we call this rustling. The conduct exhibited in these two illustrations is condemned by almost everyone the world over. But what is our attitude about a carload of high school kids who stop by a farmer's watermelon patch at 11:30 p.m. and break open two melons for a snack. The kids rationalize that the man has thirty acres of melons and that two out of the thousands there is unimportant. It is a view that their action is small and inconsequential when compared with the total picture. Some view it as having harmless fun or at worst as a youngsters' prank. Others see it as a violation of an ethical principle that places the act in the same category as car stealing or cattle rustling with the only difference being how many dollars are involved.

Those who see watermellon stealing as tolerable have, as a general rule, less trouble rationalizing a padded expense account in business or using a company car for personal use when it is in violation of company policy. One's commitment to what is "right" or willingness to tolerate deviations from "right" do not ordinarily change from the personal to the corporate areas. Our personal attitudes accompany us everywhere.

Stealing takes a number of other forms, too. As an illustration, cheating in the academic community is a form of stealing. Studies show that it is on the rise and that the rationalizations for it are as "simple" as, "Everyone is doing it," to as perverted as, "Cheating is just one way in an array of methods used to obtain information." If cheating is accepted in one's personal life then "pirating" and "stealing" a competitor's ideas—formulas, plans, designs—is its logical corporate counterpart.

Then there is the process of stealing someone's reputation through the use of innuendo, silence in the face of known error, twisted interpretation, and other such uses of information with the intent to harm. In the personal sphere it may be called gossip or "backbiting." In the corporation it may be called "politics" or the "competitive ladder." There is also bribery—an attempt to influence one's judgment so that an unfair advantage may be gained—which is still another form of attempting to steal. The reverse side of this issue is one of extortion—one will not behave ethically unless an undeserved reward is extended. Stealing does indeed take a number of forms.

The variations and implications are the same when we examine lying, causing physical harm, sexual behavior, use of language, respect for authority, and other areas of personal ethics as it is for stealing. The attitudes and values people exhibit in their personal lives will be carried over into their business roles. Business ethics is a manifestation of our personal ethics, not a separate ethical concept.

DISTRIBUTIVE JUSTICE

At the beginning of this chapter it was stated that two disjoining principles which separate people into ethical camps would be set forth and explained. The first of these principles will be presented in the form of a question—How should one deal with the issues emanating from the realities associated with human *inequality?* How one answers this question has a profound impact on a great many of our business social responsibility issues. It is the *controlling* issue in any discussion of distributive justice.

Distributive justice is concerned with the best way to distribute economic goods and services—wealth. It asks how we should determine who ought to get what proportion of the earth's scarce resources. It is an attempt to establish a normative principle that will guide people in their search for a *just* system of distribution. The world, however, is divided on its answer. There are four theories that dominate men's thinking—these will be briefly defined—but the watershed or disjoining issue revolves around how people deal with the concepts and realities of human equality and inequality.

How are we to distribute economic wealth? Culturally there are two theories of normative justice offered as solutions to the question. They are: (1) normative justice requires that distribution be made according to people's "rights" and "natural equality"—this is called the "fairness" principle; and (2) normative justice requires that distribution be made according to what people are "due" or "owed" which is determined by their "natural inequality"—referred to as the "due" principle.

If the above is so, then how do we determine what each person's "rights" are or what each is "due?" The "fairness" ("rights") principle offers two possible answers: (a) each person should receive an *equal* share; or (b) each person should receive a share according to his or her *need*. This is so because people are "naturally equal." The "due" principle offers three bases for resolving the question: (1) each person should receive an amount reflecting his or her *effort;* (2) each is due a share according to his *contribution;* or (3) distribution should be made on a basis of *merit.* These principles are said to be best because they reflect our "natural inequality."

The four predominant theories of distributive justice that reflect and incorporate the above concepts of distribution are: egalitarianism; Marxism; libertarianism; and utilitarianism.[1] We will examine each of these very briefly and then move to an examination of the disjoining principle that flows from our treatment of *natural equality* and *natural inequality.*

Egalitarianism is a philosophy espousing the equality of humans

[1] Tom L. Beauchamp and Norman E. Bowie, eds., *Ethical Theory and Business,* (New Jersey: Prentice-Hall, Inc., 1979) pp. 29-121.

with regard to social, political, and economic rights. It goes even a step further and advocates the removal of certain inequalities that exist between people. Probably the clearest and most profound modern discourse on this subject is contained in the work of John Rawls entitled *A Theory of Justice.*[2] He presumes that one should hold, in a normative system of distributive justice, that inequalities between individuals reflecting intellectual, physical, or experience differences are in fact *undeserved* differences. Social, political, and economic theory should, in all fairness, according to Rawls, assume that all cooperative action among men is between equals. So, minimally, society should provide equal access to all primary goods. Egalitarianism emphasizes the "fairness" of equality and the "undeservedness" of inequality.

Marxism is a philosophy grounded in a view of the nature of man that holds all men to be innately creative in a manner, except when alienated from themselves, that looks to the fostering of a *common* life. Unalienated human nature will, according to Marx, strive to produce an "authentic common life" which flows from the very needs and ego of every individual. But Marx perceived that the individual man was becoming more and more alienated from himself and that this deterioration in the human spirit was directly related to the rise of capitalism. The more successful capitalism was, the more men became wage earners who specialized on a narrow task at work. This task orientation was, according to Marx, destroying the holistic view of work as a creative self expression and thus men were becoming alienated from their work (themselves). Marx therefore advocated the abolition of private property—the mark of individual alienation—and the resurgence of the state (common life). For Marx, the rise of individualism, which was reflective of men's alienation, would result in classes of people—a result of human inequality—alienated from one another. This was inhuman in his eyes. According to Marx, human satisfaction should flow from one's creative work, and not from the distribution of the resulting wealth. Inequality should be reflected in people's creative work but not in the arena of distribution. Wealth should be distributed on a basis of *need* where the common good is taken into consideration. "Equality" is a central value to be sought in this system.

---

[2] John A. Rawls, *A Theory of Justice,* (Mass.: Harvard University Press, 1971).

Libertarianism for many is equated with the concept of "laissez-faire." Negatively this is a position advocating no government beyond the minimum necessary for the maintenance of personal property and peace. Positively it advocates individual freedom in matters of thought and action so long as one's personal actions do not infringe on the personal freedom of a neighbor. Here individualism is propounded. Personal responsibility is emphasized. The freedom to exercise one's volitional will is championed. This philosophy believes that everyone benefits from the encouragement of individual, creative, human endeavor that allows for the full development of one's unique abilities and talents—inequality of individuals. Under this view, everyone should reap all of the consequences—positive and negative—for his or her individual life's expression (laziness or hard work). Natural inequality should be allowed to run its natural course.

Utilitarianism is a philosophy that focuses on actions and does not speak about motives. Jeremy Bentham and John Stuart Mill were two of its major proponents and it was the dominant normative ethical doctrine in the industrial west during the 19th century. Under this philosophy, actions are accepted as the correct ones when they produce the "most net good" when compared with other alternatives. Here, the reality that a "good" may produce some consequential harm is admitted (accepted), but so long as the "good" results outweigh the negative ones, the act is accepted as good. When two or more actions could produce a "net good" (the good outweighs the bad) then the one creating the "most net good" is deemed to be the best. The fact that some may be injured while others are helped is accepted as part of the reality. Many have liked this philosophy because they viewed it as logical (to the quantitative, scientific mind), socially beneficial to the majority, "natural" in its character, and *neutral* in matters of distributive justice. But in fact it is only silent and *not* neutral in matters of distributive justice. *It is natural but not neutral.* Those with positive inequalities have natural advantages over those with negative inequalities. Implicitly, utilitarianism favors inequality over equality.

We can summarize as follows:

A. How are we to distribute economic goods and services?

According to "rights" and "natural equality" (Principles of "Fairness") or

Normative Justice

According to "due", "owed," and "natural inequality" (Principles of "Due")

B. What should each person get?
   1. By Principles of "Fairness":
      a. To each an *equal* share
      b. To each according to *need*, or
   2. By Principle of "Due":
      a. To each according to *effort*
      b. To each according to *contribution*
      c. To each according to *merit*

C. Theories of Distributive Justice and What They Emphasize:
   1. Egalitarianism: equality; removal of inequality (undeserved in nature); equal access to all primary goods; seek equality in the distribution of wealth.
   2. Marxism: unalienated natural man wants a common life; wages alienate man from his work; abolition of private property; inequality should only exist in work, not distribution; distribute according to need.
   3. Libertarianism: personal freedom; private property; individualism; personal responsibility and consequences; natural inequality.
   4. Utilitarianism: emphasizes actions (not motives); seeks "most net good"; natural in character; favors positive inequalities.

An examination of the theories of distributive justice quickly reveals the central importance of, and disjoining impact of, choosing to emphasize either the aspects of natural human equality or natural human inequality. This is one of the two disjoining ethical selections that confront any ethicist dealing with issues of corporate social responsibility. We need to look now at the content of what is embodied in the concepts of human equality and inequality. (A review of Chapter 3 would prove helpful at this point.)

In what ways are humans equal? Without wanting to sound trite or dwell on the self-evident, it must be said that whatever general worth, respect, and dignity that should accrue to any individual by virtue of the fact that he or she is a human should automatically be attached to any other human. Or, put another way, one human being is not less of a human than another one. There are natural equalities in human worth and dignity. Our "Bill of Rights" (Constitutional) speaks of equality under the law, the right to hold private property, the right to pursue happiness, and other such areas of human equality as expressed in their "rights."

In what ways are humans unequal? It is evident that individuals have different intellectual capacities, abilities, and interests. It is further evident that people have different abilities with regard to strength, dexterity, and mobility, not to mention that we enter life in one of two sexual forms. In addition, we are very unequal in our experiences which cover a host of differences ranging from the kind of family we were born in; our cultural exposure; our opportunities to travel; educational; and many others. There are many natural inequalities.

When we look back at the diagram in Chapter 2 that shows the outline of the Reformational/Renaissance Ethic, the God/Man Ethic, that had its roots deeply embedded in the Judaic/Christian perception of reality, we will remember that this ethic perceived that equality *and* inequality were both positive aspects of human reality. And when we examine the Empiricist/Rationalist/Existentialist Ethic, the Man Ethic, we discover that equality alone is viewed as a positive dimension of the human experience. Under this ethic the aspects of inequality that affect human endeavors are perceived as undeserved. So the debate boils down to what one thinks about *inequality*. Our disjoining principle is discovered when we face the question: "How should one deal with the issues emanating from the realities associated with human inequality?

The answer to this question rests upon what we discussed in Chapters 4 through 6 (How Do We Determine True Truth?), and one's justification base (discussed in Chapter 8). Every decision maker *must* resolve this question to his or her own satisfaction before trying to tackle real world social responsibility questions. Furthermore, it must be remembered that a choice—either one— will bring with it a set of consequences that will be rejected by many others in our ethically schizophrenic society.

In trying to resolve such a "bedrock" question, matters such as the "nature of man"; do individuals have a "free will"; is there a God; what is God's nature and will; what are human rights; what are our human responsibilities; what is our destiny; do we have purpose and meaning; and a number of other questions and their perceived answers underlie our choice and emphasis.

CORPORATE
MORALITY

So far in this chapter we have discussed
the fact that our personal values are the
ones we bring to our jobs and apply to
the issues we face there—personal and business ethics have the
same genesis. And we have examined the basic issues associated
with distributive justice and the disjoining choice associated with
resolving whether or not human inequality should be treated as a
negative or positive natural reality. Now we want to turn to the
third and last concept to be covered in this chapter—"Who is morally responsible for the corporation's behavior?" The answer to
this question produces our second disjoining principle—the selection between a *private* or *public* property answer with all of its accompanying consequences.

In developing an answer to this question—Who is *morally* responsible for the corporation?—the first step is to answer still
another question: Are the same people (or entities) responsible for
the moral activities of a corporation as are responsible for the financial and legal activities and obligations of a corporation? There
is more "fuzzy" thinking on the answer to this question than any
other one in the study of corporate social responsibility. And the
kind of collective answer we give will determine the very character
of our society in the future. How is this so?

In 1866 the American corporations were declared to be a "person" in the eyes of the law. An entity, a "thing," was given the
status of a human with all of the rights and privileges associated
with such a position. This new status was not accompanied, however, with a declaration concerning any corresponding duties or
responsibilities. The "thing" (corporation) was now a "person"
and could act as such in both *legal* and *financial* matters. In the
same breath, those who owned, directed, and managed the corporation were declared to have limited financial and legal liability.
From now on one's financial liability was limited to the extent of
his immediate financial investment in the individual entity. The
entity had unlimited liability but not so its directors and managers.
Suddenly executives became agents of an "artificial being."

Who then is *morally* responsible for this artificial being—the
corporation? To answer, the same "one" is morally responsible
that is financially and legally responsible is to say a nonmoral entity
(corporation) is morally responsible. That is an illogical answer but
one that is widely held. An inanimate "thing" cannot by law or
any other human act be transformed into a moral being. A corpor-

ation cannot, and thus does not, have a moral character. Then who is morally responsible for it?

First we need to list the possible candidates for the honor of having this responsibility placed on them. The candidates are: the corporation (illogical or not); the corporate owners (stockholders); corporate directors; corporate managers; the general public; and government (legally prescribed agencies). Each of the above nominees has its rooting section and its detractors. Let us look at each of them, one at a time.

For almost eighty years (1866-1946), no one who bothered to ask who was morally responsible for our corporations could even find an influential audience that thought the question merited their interest. Why so little interest for so many years and then the surge of concern over the past several decades? The answer rests in the fact that we had a high degree of ethical consensus in our culture for those first eighty years and that has been shattered over the past thirty-five years. So what the corporation did through its directors and managers was not generally upsetting to the public or those who governed. Because of this many people simply grew to accept (implicitly) that the *corporation* was morally responsible for its own actions. It was, legally and financially. Why not morally? As stated two paragraphs earlier, an inanimate thing cannot be considered moral in any ethical sense of the word.

There are still plenty of people, however, (owners, directors, and managers in particular) who insist that the corporation is morally responsible for its own actions. This is claimed to be so by these groups, not on a basis of logic but because the alternatives— directors and managers are, or the government is responsible—are not acceptable to them. For those who own, direct, or manage the corporation to say "we" are morally responsible for our corporation's actions opens the door for potential consequential repercussions that are simply unacceptable to them. The safety screen of "limited liability" could be ripped away if such an admission were made. The alternative is equally repulsive to them. In no way do the owners, directors, or managers want to appoint the general public, or those who govern, responsible for the corporation's actions. That would reflect a radical shift in our values that would manifest itself in a new power and reward base within our society. So we still have many people who claim that the corporation is morally responsible for itself in an effort to avoid personal consequences.

Unaffected people do not mind when others claim that the corporation is morally responsible for itself, but affected people do, because they are looking for *people* who can bring about change. People who believe that corporations are not acting responsibly in certain areas and who are frustrated in their dealings with managers who deny any moral responsibility soon come to view corporate managers as the "Wizards of Biz." They are analogous to the Wizard of Oz. At the beginning of this century a work was published that was entitled *The Wizard of Oz*. One of its central characters. Oz the Great and Terrible, was afraid of the people in the Land of Oz so he sat behind a screen in the throne room pulling levers and strings while performing as a ventriloquist. He did this in order to maintain a safe position from which he could act with authority and presume responsibility while avoiding accountability. He wanted the benefits of the position but wanted to avoid the possible consequences that could become associated with it.[3]

Corporate directors and managers in particular are seen by many as our modern day Wizards of Biz. They seem to want the authority and responsibility associated with their positions while renouncing their accountability. When directors and managers act with authority (tell others what to do); assume responsibility (the right and obligation to determine what act is the appropriate one); but turn and say that the corporation is morally responsible for itself (corporation is consequentially accountable) then those who differ with the corporation's actions feel a deep frustration. Owners, directors, and managers all hide behind the screen of limited liability while wanting the rewards, prestige, and power associated with such leadership and ownership. But they do not want to be *consequentially accountable*—a condition where others judge our performance and have the right, effective power, and willingness to reward, correct, or remove us for our actions. None of them want to emerge from behind the "screen" and accept moral accountability.

The owners, while legally responsible under the law for the corporation, are certainly not effectively responsible. They are scattered, financially weak (compared to the corporation's net worth), disorganized, and ineffective in the power structure (meaningful influence on the board and management). Even the proxy mechanism of electing directors makes the board self perpetuating. Power groups within the organization may fear one another but they rarely

[3] L. Frank Baum, *The Wizard of Oz*, (Indianapolis: The Bobbs-Merrill Company, 1903) pp. 142-155.

fear the stockholders. So the owners are not the best candidates to have the responsibility for the corporation's moral conduct assigned to them.

The debate on whether or not the corporation can be rightly declared to be morally responsible for itself—the author holds that it cannot—will not be debated further here, but if no humans from the private property side of the debate will step forward and assume the moral responsibility for our corporations, then the question (issue) will ultimately be resolved through a power struggle. People who differ with corporations' actions will not long be put off by their opponent's pointing a finger at a "thing" and blaming "it." The disgruntled will want access to those who make the "things" act. If this is legally denied them, then in time they will seek direct control of the "things" (corporations) and transform them into public property.

For those who believe that the moral responsibility for corporations' actions must rest with people, then they are left to choose between owners (not a good candidate), directors, managers, the public, or those who govern. Now our second disjoining principle quickly comes to light. Our choice is between a "private" or "public" property solution. This is the second big social issue. While there are some serious and practical issues wrapped up in the debates over whether owners or directors/managers should be held morally responsible for their corporations—they generally do not want to be held morally accountable. The disjoining question is whether the moral responsibility for corporations should be shouldered by those in the private sector or borne by those in the public sector of our society.

The principle under debate is indeed a disjoining one. And what is at stake is the maintenance of a concept of private property or the further evolvement of the concept that our corporations ought to be public property. The matter is not an academic one. The question is once again, like the discussion on "inequality," a bedrock one that quickly touches many of the basic concepts about human nature, human rights, and human responsibilities. Are we all best served in the long-run by casting our efforts behind a system of private property, controlled by private citizens, making private decisions, whose actions are morally their responsibility, and who will privately reap the rewards and/or suffer the remediating consequences associated with their personal choices and actions? Or, are we benefited most in the long-run by supporting a system of public property, controlled by governing bodies who make decisions on behalf of the public. And will these people assume personal, moral responsibility for their decisions and want to be held personally accountable in a consequential system of rewards and penalties? (Those on the public or governing side of these discussions have shown no more zeal for assuming personal, consequential accountability than those in the private sector.)

CORPORATE SOCIAL RESPONSIBILITY So far we have discussed the following: (a) our personal values are the basis for our business values; (b) the disjoining principle associated with distributive justice—how do we deal with the natural realities associated with human inequality; and (c) the disjoining principle associated with the issues surrounding corporate morality—do we champion the placing of the moral responsibility for corporate behavior on the shoulders of our private sector, operating on the basis of private property, or do we want the public sector to assume effective control of our corporate property? Having done this, we are now ready to address the big question: What are the social responsibilities of corporations? This text will not answer the question—how could it even presume to when we are living in an ethically schizophrenic society where a consensus is impossible to achieve—but we will look at the steps one must follow and the questions one must answer to his or her own satisfaction as an answer to the question is formulated by the individual. The following is an ordered five-step procedure for determining corporate social responsibility:

I. Define and consequentially live with a principled set of personal values.
II. *Question:* Are the mass of people constituting a society best served and enabled to achieve: (a) personal development of their potential; (b) enlargement of their creative expression through human endeavor; (c) maintenance of maximal human choice; (d) the enhancement of human dignity; and (e) the pursuit of happiness, through a system that puts its emphasis on the enhancement of the *individual* or the *group*?
Answers: Our system of *distributive justice* is directly affected by our choice of answers—individual or group.

   A. Choosing an emphasis on the *individual* will lead to the concept of normative justice (distributive) that emphasizes "natural inequality" in human intellectual, physical, and experience matters while seeing "natural equality" as pertaining to the treatment due people by other humans and the state in matters of social and political justice. (Distributive justice is a function of a *market mechanism* reflecting free human choice.)

   B. Choosing to emphasize the *group* leads to the normative concept of "natural equality" (distributive) where the consequences of "natural inequality" are perceived to be undeserved and counter to certain basic "human rights"—entitlements. (Distributive justice should reflect group choice as embodied in the *law*—redistribution of wealth—and not as accomplished in the market place.)

III. *Question:* Who is *morally* responsible for the corporation?
Answers: The possibilities for an answer rest on the following: (a) directors; (b) managers; (c) owners; (d) public (society); or (e) government. (The "corporation" has intentionally been left off the list.)

   A. Selecting (a), (b), and/or (c) leads to the concept of holding the corporation to be *private property*.

   B. Selecting (d) and/or (e) results in considering the corporation to be effectively *public property*.

Consequences: The selection of A or B as an answer has profound consequences upon the following issues that are related to corporate social responsibility: (1) the corporate *social contract*; and (2) corporate *responsibility, authority, and accountability*—from where are they derived; and for what ends are they to be used?

IV. The Corporate Social Contract:
When people speak of the corporation's "social contract," they are conversing about the fact that all corporations derive their existence, rights, and protection from within the republicanly-derived framework of government wherein the general citizenry is entitled to determine how the affairs of state are to be conducted. In other words, in a democratic state the people have the right to determine the privileges and limits imposed on all institutions. As a people we reserve the right to emphasize the use of private property concepts in the affairs

of business; to limit the use of private property (effectively moving it toward public property); or of outright nationalizing business property so as to make it public property. Historically we sided heavily with the concepts of private property. Today we are divided but have moved substantially toward the regulation of private property so as to effectively direct it in many areas of its conduct as if it were public property. Answering the question, who is morally responsible for the corporation, substantially determines the resolution of which basic building block a society will operate from—private property or public property. The value (which is right or wrong) associated with this basic issue is a foundational one. When we couple our solution to this issue—*private or public property*—with our *personal values* and our conclusions on the merits or demerits relative to the consequences flowing from human *inequality*, we have the essentials necessary to determine, from our personal perspective, what a corporation's social responsibility ought to be. (Remember, our society has lost its basis for formulating a consensus on all of this.)

V. Corporate Responsibility, Authority, and Accountability— Their Derivations and Their Ends:

If one emerges on the side that favors "private property," then corporate responsibility, authority, and accountability rest with those who are morally responsible for it—directors, managers, and/or owners. Those who are morally responsible are responsible for determining their corporation's social responsibility. The public's recourses are to: (a) accept the actions of the corporation; (b) sue for harm (irresponsible actions); or (c) rewrite the social contract through legislation and move even closer to the concepts of public property. If, on the other hand, one chooses to work for the further development of the concepts of public property, then those who are morally responsible for the corporation's actions—legislators, regulators, and other public authorities—must be subject also to the consequences associated with accountability. They must be consequentially available and subject to either the ballot box or the courts. But either choice—private or public property—is profoundly tied to the issues of human development, creativity, choice, motivation, dignity, and happiness.

CONCLUSION   Whether one is debating about the issues
                        and values associated with the problems
                        of discrimination, protection of the en-
vironment, employee health and safety, self regulation versus government regulation, product safety, or a host of other topics, if
the discussants will identify their basic personal values, work
through and accept their consequential stand on the matters of
human inequality, and be willing to commit to a defense of the
private or public property concepts with all of their ramifications,
then and only then can they meaningfully address and answer the
questions associated with the issues surrounding the corporation's
social responsibility. As an illustration, if the reader believes that
the wealth differences between people associated with our system
of economic distribution are unjust and undeserved, then there is
a much stronger appeal associated with the concepts of public
property. If, on the other hand, one puts individual efforts above
group "rights" on a value scale, then policies of "nondiscrimination" will generally be more appealing to such a person than those
calling for "affirmative action." Our perceptions on these basics
shape our conclusions on almost all of the social responsibility
questions.

Our perceptions of the basics—personal values; equality/inequal-
ity; and private versus public property—are directly related to our
deepest ethical values which were discussed in the earlier chapters.
The reader might profitably once again briefly scan the two major
contrasting ethics set forth on pages 18 and 19 and relate them in
his or her own mind to the topic of business social responsibility.
Which of those ethics should our culture hold? Chapters 4-6 explained the development of our culture's ethical schizophrenia
which results in our inability to develop a consensus in answering
such a question. Then we turned to an examination of how we
could identify where we and others are ethically. This determination is necessary for purposes of: understanding; communication;
making possible effective compromise; and other such aspects of
human endeavor so vital in such a diverse society. Then in Chapter
8 we examined the necessity for, and process of, defending one's
ethical posture. This justification process was described as the
"bottom of the well" of our ethical understanding. It is the last
line of defense. It is the best we can do.

This chapter has been designed to relate, in a specific way, how business leaders can come to grips with the big issues associated with our businesses' social responsibilities. This was done through looking at some underlying principles that divide our people There is not likely to be any consensus on what business ought to do, however. We are badly divided. We have different values. We are ethically schizophrenic.

Given that so many ethical differences do exist in our culture, are there any practical guides to assist people of every persuasion who genuinely desire to be ethical? Yes!

BIBLIOGRAPHY

Arthur, John; and William H. Shaw, eds., *Justice and Economic Distribution.* Englewood Cliffs, New Jersey: Prentice-Hall, 1978.

Beauchamp, Tom L.; and Norman E. Bowie, *Ethical Theory and Business.* Englewood Cliffs, New Jersey: Prentice-Hall, 1979.

DeGeorge, Richard T.; and Joseph A. Pichler, eds., *Ethics, Free Enterprise, and Public Policy: Original Essays on Moral Issues in Business.* New York: Oxford University Press, 1978.

Friedman, Milton, *Capitalism and Freedom.* Chicago: University of Chicago Press, 1962.

Harrington, Michael, *Socialism.* New York: Saturday Review Press, 1972.

Rawls, John, *A Theory of Justice.* Cambridge, Mass.: Harvard University Press, 1971.

Steiner, George A., *Business and Society.* (2nd edition). New York: Random House, 1975.

CHAPTER

TEN

PRACTICAL GUIDES

CHAOS AND ORDER   It is evident by now that our culture is in a state of ethical schizophrenia—unable to develop an ethical consensus. We are at ethical odds within and between groups. Many individuals have inner conflicts and unresolved tensions. Some say we are "going to the dogs." Others say we are merely in a period of transition and will emerge with a new ethic that will be acceptable to the vast majority of our people. And there are those who declare that everything is normal and that every generation sees itself as being in a period of radical change.

The proposed solutions for the perceived problems are as varied as are the views about our basic condition. There are those who believe the government must legislate and regulate a standard of public conduct. There are others who decry this on the grounds that those making the laws or writing the regulatory guidelines have no more insight into what is proper and just than anyone else. Why give a select group the responsibility? And anyway, how do you select the select group? There are those who point to the intellectual community and say that it is from this group that our help must come. Others counter that it was from within this group that the problem was given birth and this is the most divergent and fractured body of all. The intellectuals' critics say that those who are in chaos themselves should not be looked to for solutions until their own house is in order. Some believe that only an old fashioned revival, which would effectively bring everyone to their knees before God to repent and cause us to seek his Biblically revealed will, is capable of restoring harmony to our views and beliefs. Still others hold that these ethical differences can be resolved in a free system where people register their choices by the expenditure of their dollars. The answer according to them is less government, less regulation, and more freedom to exercise personal and group choices on an unencumbered basis. Others counter this by saying that the old system had its chance and exhibited so many deficiencies during the past fifty years that it cannot be trusted. Self control and good judgment were too often lacking. The lesser good was too often chosen. So these critics do not see more freedom of choice as a viable option.

The only opinion that seems acceptable to the majority is the bland understatement that there is a growing ethical problem with no apparent ready solution on the horizon. If this is true, then the question needs to be asked, "Are there any practical steps that can be taken by individuals who desire to be ethical, regardless of their specific ethical presuppositions, that will reduce the chaos and help in establishing harmony and order?" Yes, there are. The following fourteen concepts are independent of any particular ethical system. They are, however, related to the beliefs that social interaction is aided by *order*; that the *dignity* of one person is as important as the dignity of another; and that people are ethically *responsible* for their relationships.

ETHICAL COMMITMENT
Until a person perceives that "being" and "doing" what is right is really important to him, no amount of moralizing will have any substantial impact. One human cannot persuade another one to make a deep and genuine commitment to seek what is "right." In fact, no one can explain their own ethical commitment with any more persuasion than they can their base of ethical justification—the two go together—and we learned earlier (Chapter 8) that we do not *prove* our basis of justification.

Some people, however, are ethically committed while others are not. There are degrees of commitment, but those that are have a special opportunity to be constructively influential. Our culture has many examples of Chief Executive Officers who are deeply committed to being ethical, and the organizations they head reflect this same posture. When ethically committed leadership reveals its desire for ethical behavior, through both personal action and communication, those under them tend to assume the standards! In any hierarchy, the example set by the leaders—ethical or unethical—becomes the tone for the group. Once the tone is set, it takes an extra measure of gumption—positive or negative—to go against the mainstream or flow of the group. Business leaders, as leaders in any field, can have a tremendous positive ethical influence on the organizations they lead. This is also true for leaders at every level within an organization.

As mentioned earlier, our problem is not so much in knowing what is right as it is in doing what is right. Our ideas about what is normatively right can and do come into conflict with our "self will," and the immediate short-term rewards that can accompany a particular questionable opportunity that may produce real temptations for us to choose the lesser good. The "self will" can easily seem "best" in the face of the normative "right." The "best" is before us in a tangible opportunity that appears to be rather certain. The normative "right" can seem so far away, intangible, and problematic at the moment. It is easy to understand how the rationalization mechanism gets set in motion under such conditions. Understanding this about ourselves and being committed to the "right" beforehand is the only hope anyone has of meeting and conquering the temptation of choosing the lesser good when it presents itself.

Another thing that is very important in this regard is to maintain associations with peers and superiors who are ethically committed themselves. Choosing associates who are ethical provides basic support to all who want to do what is "right" and reduces the opportunities and temptations to pick the lesser good. There is strength in numbers when there is mutual support and recognition.

FACTS AND EVIDENCE

Accurate, factual information is imperative to have if good ethical decisions are to be made. Facts do shape our perceptions. Facts are the descriptive bounds of reality. They are the raw materials for human judgment. Each fact is like a piece of a puzzle.

The more pieces you have in place, the better idea you have of what the whole picture looks like. Always get as many facts as practically possible, within the constraints of the time available, before formulating a judgment.

Facts alone do not provide the qualitative elements necessary for ethics, but they do set the scene within which the ethical judgments must be rendered, carried out, and interpreted. When making judgments about people, the information gathered should, where possible, reflect the individual's actions over a period of time and in a variety of circumstances. Look for patterns that may provide *converging evidence.* Always hesitate before making a judgment that is based on an event or incident. Anyone who does things makes errors of judgment. Is the evidence, negative or positive, reflected in a number of situations or is it isolated in character? Be cautious in the use of isolated evidence.

And always be careful with second hand evidence concerning a person. The decision maker may be getting second and third hand reports which are carriers of implied or explicit judgments (not just facts) which bring weights, nuances, and biases to the color of the report. People who are responsible for passing along such reports should know that they, the reporters, are being evaluated on the accuracy of their perceptions and reports as well.

Another general principle is that a decision maker who finds it necessary to deal with conflicts between subordinates should never make a judgment before the parties have been required to sit together, face to face, and work on their differences. If this fails to resolve the conflict, then make sure that both positions are presented accurately and fairly to the person resolving the conflict. Decisions affecting people obviously need to be fair and just in character, but final judgments need to be carefully and fully communicated and explained to all parties affected. Make every judgment with as much background information as it is reasonably possible to get.

COUNSEL   When one desires to be ethical, good counsel can be of tremendous benefit.

First of all, by simply communicating the circumstances and situation surrounding an impending decision to someone else, the decision maker finds it necessary to organize, structure, explain, and relate the entire matter. This process alone will inevitably bring about a measure of clarification and an expanded understanding of the situation as a byproduct of the exercise. If no other benefits beside this were gained, this alone would still make the exercise very worthwhile. The counseling setting provides a safe environment in which ideas, thoughts, and concerns can be expressed without having to make a commitment to them. In counsel, expressions are preliminary in nature. Sometimes simply hearing the idea verbalized helps us evaluate it in a way that merely thinking about it does not. The time of counsel is a time to test our ideas and not a time to finalize them.

In seeking a counselor, when ethical ramifications are a concern, find a person who is ethically committed and who has a justification base that is compatible with, or at least appreciative of, the posture of your own. There must be an atmosphere that is free of judgment and where an open exchange is natural and comfortable. This allows for the "turning" of a decision so that its many facets can be considered. This provides an opportunity to order the priorities, which is critical and essential in all decision making.

A good adviser may be found among one's peers, superiors, subordinates, family or friends. Their position does not determine their ability to give good counsel. Their ability to listen; their astuteness in raising clarifying questions; their ability to identify critical issues; their ability to encourage the "right" choice and support the decision maker are the more critical characteristics to find.

Good counsel builds confidence; brings encouragement; helps develop resolve to do what is right, even if it will prove difficult; and produces better decisions.

**MULTIPLE
TRACKS**
People who really desire to be ethical should cultivate the habit of testing themselves and their decisions and actions on more than one of the ethical paths. One needs to ask, "Is this *action* good in itself and/or does it have a good consequence?" In addition, decision makers ought to ask themselves, "Does the decision come from and reflect a *trait* of character or *motive* that is good in itself and/or produces a good consequence?" (These two questions cover the "multiple ethical tracks" as discussed in Chapter 7.)

Multiple track testing—seeking positive answers to every aspect of the two questions just raised—causes us to turn the decision around under the ethical light and look for ethical flaws from more than just one angle. It also forces decision makers to examine their personal motives and intentions that are related to, and prone to affect, decisions. Anyone acting as an agent (corporate decision makers acting in the name of the corporation) needs this kind of check to examine his or her rationalization process. It is easy to assume, or want to believe, that what is best for me now is also best for the corporation in the long-run. Often that is not true. When it is not, the process of examining our motives on the multiple ethical tracks can be very helpful in surfacing, clarifying, and handling the temptation to choose the lesser good. When managers are acting for owners, whose true interests should be advanced, then the managers need to examine their own motives often since they are operating from a position of trust.

As stated earlier, there is "what" we decide to do and there is the "how" we are going to carry it out. At the attitudinal, interpersonal level of decision making, the "ethics of being" (traits and motives) is especially critical, but those in the business community often think of and treat this dimension as if it were limited to the sphere of personal ethics. This is a false dichotomy. *Every person in business is an ethical center and an influential force.* Furthermore, most personnel evaluations rest explicitly on objective, functional performance evaluations but everyone acknowledges privately that there is always present, and inherent, an implicit subjective personality dimension to the evaluation—in the academic world we call it collegiality. This personal dimension of ethics is deeply involved in the "politics" of any organization. It generally constitutes a good portion of the subjective evaluation that lies behind the interpretation of the objective facts.

DECISIONS AND   A good ethical decision, which is related
IMPLEMENTATION   to a major business choice, can be under-
                         mined as it is implemented by those who
carry it out. Using philosophical language, a "good end" needs to be accompanied and carried out by "good means," if it is to be widely accepted. A major decision once reached—build a new plant, purchase a noncompetitive supplier—will be the generator of literally thousands of secondary decisions and actions whose

potential impact will range from being very serious in character to being inconsequential.

So, coming to an ethical position in the decision making process is only the first step in being ethical. Each and every step must be viewed as part of an ethical fabric. Just as there are the words people use in speaking to one another, there is also the tone and inflection of our words along with the body language that is used in delivering the message. Often the tone, inflection, and body language carry an even bigger message than the words themselves. And so it is with ethics. The true spirit of the major decision is lived and discovered in the implementation process. How we treat the minor situations and people under us will generally provide a pretty good barometer of our ethical sensitivity.

PREPARATORY & Uncertainty is a condition that gives rise
PREVENTATIVE to tension which, in turn, is often mani-
ETHICS fested in less than ethical human con-
duct. Ethical behavior is deeply affected by our *expectations.* A great many of our interpersonal perceptions (judgments) are directly related to our having unfulfilled or satisfied expectations. This being the case, there is an ethical imperative that those in positions of authority inform their subordinates of the expectations they are living under. In addition to informing them of what is expected, those being evaluated need to be informed on a reasonably frequent basis if those expectations are being met inadequately, minimally, sufficiently, very well, or in a superior manner. Without some kind of reference point, the person being judged has no way of knowing how he is being perceived and evaluated.

It is truly unethical to fire someone, apart from a flagrant violation of known norms, until the superior can affirm that the unfulfilled expectation was known by the offending party and that observed deficiencies had been adequately communicated and worked with, prior to severing the employment. Supervisors who do not have the courage or ethical sensitivity to confront unacceptable conditions in a constructive manner, prior to their total deterioration, are inadequate themselves for their responsibility.

Having a full disclosure of expectations is the best single way of preparing all parties for a good working relationship and of preventing serious breakdowns that need remediation or radical action. The use of a nonpersonal rationalization like, "Our business is slack, and while I hate to do it, I must let you go," is an unethical procedure (not true) and destructive to the human dignity (not constructively corrective) when used as a cover for someone's poor performance.

**ETHICS OF
ANGER**

What do you do with anger in a business setting? Some people say that anger should be suppressed. Others say it should be expressed. But if so, how? Being humans and not automated machines, anger is a part of our life's experience. We must keep functioning ethically and soundly, even when angry. This is not nearly as hard as people think it is.

There are those who recommend golf—go and hit the ball. Some suggest changing the subject by restimulating the mind and redirecting it to a new subject. But none of these are effective in ridding ourselves of the long range feelings associated with anger. If we do not deal with it properly, it stays inside of us and attaches itself to some other "safe" target and gets misplaced. Redirecting anger is not a good long-run solution for handling it.

Anger must be properly placed if it is to be effectively expressed. If Bill is angry with Jim, he will not rid himself of the anger by telling Bob, Mary, and Henry about it. That serves as a temporary release for the "steam" but does not get rid of the emotion or its effects. Bill must relate his anger to Jim to affect any constructive result. But that does not imply that he must express his anger in an angry manner or attack Jim in a degrading fashion. Anger must be expressed in a constructive way so as to benefit all parties, if it is to be done ethically. How can this be done?

There is a simple formula for dealing with anger. It can be expressed abbreviatedly as "I" . . . "When" . . . "Because." The process is simple. Avoid the use of the pronoun "you" when confronting the person who has made you angry. Statements like, "You have really made me angry," will immediately bring forth all of the defenses that the second party can muster. As soon as people hear "you," they begin protecting themselves. This is rarely constructive and will generally slow up or prevent a healing, even if the party being confronted is absolutely wrong. The desire is to have them first recognize and then accept the responsibility for their inappropriate words or acts. So the offended party should and can safely draw attention to his own hurt or disappointment by starting with a statement that identifies his own personal feelings—"I am really upset about not being told that the shipment would be three days late in going out." Here the attention is drawn to the feelings of the offended party and no accusations have been leveled at anyone. The feeling is out in the open.

Next the offended party should immediately proceed to explain why such feelings were forthcoming, by relating the circumstances—"when"—that gave birth to the emotional response. "*I* am really upset about not being told that the shipment would be three days late in going out. *When* I have promised a customer that I will have a shipment on the way on a certain date. . . ." Finally, the reason—"because"—is stated, which is the heart of the problem. "*I* am really upset about not being told that the shipment would be three days late in going out. *When* I have promised a customer that I will have a shipment on the way on a certain date, and it fails to occur, I boil *because* it makes me and the whole organization appear to be unreliable and subjects us to the possible loss of future orders for being undependable."

The emotion is out; the circumstances are reviewed; the reason is stated; and no one has been accused. The person hearing this may "own" the problem; shift responsibility to someone else—even back to the angry person by reminding him of a procedure which he failed to follow when entering a rush order; or alibi. But anger handled in this way is ethically employed. It holds people accountable and responsible for the exercise of their authority without being demeaning or avoiding the reality.

ETHICS OF SILENCE   To consciously refuse to make a decision in business, or in any walk of life, is in fact to have made a decision. In the same way, to be intentionally silent in the face of events is as full of ethical implications as making statements and directing actions. One does not escape ethical responsibility by keeping quiet. There are a number of circumstances that could be used to illustrate this point, but three should be sufficient.

There are those situations where we have helpful knowledge and find others coming to a misleading conclusion or taking actions that will not be constructive, due to their lack of information. To keep silent in the face of this is to participate in the conclusions or events. To purposefully allow falsity to prevail is to condone or share in it. Second, to be part of a group that comes to an unethical conclusion and remain silent, after personally concluding that the proposed course is morally inappropriate, is, in reality, to concur with the decision behaviorally. And finally, to provide partial truth to a person on the one hand while remaining silent about other potentially influential facts is to intentionally lead another to a potentially inappropriate conclusion. Such silence is no better than a lie. This is intentionally misleading and the willful acceptance of a lesser good for someone else than you would want for yourself. A person's dignity has been intentionally violated. This is unethical. "Silence is golden" only when it does no harm.

TOLERANCE AND SELF RESPECT   This entire treatise has been devoted to showing the major and sharp differences that do exist between those who have different perspectives on ethical issues. How are the majority and minority to face one another when the differences have been aired but not resolved? The confrontation of two opposing wills is fraught with ethical considerations. Our volitional will is often thinly veiled at such a time.

Social order requires bounded freedom. Having one's freedom within defined bounds necessitates self control (discipline) and the acceptance of the necessity of societal limits. There also needs to be a process whereby grievances may be redressed or denied in the face of some group's claim when one party perceives that the existing social bounds are unjust or too limiting. Given all of this there are still thwarted wills and grieved consciences. Differences are real and consequential. How are they to be lived with?

An overworked but often misunderstood appeal is the call for *tolerance* when sharp differences are being aired. Tolerance is accepting a deviation from a standard or norm and adjusting to the variance. Tolerance is only a viable option until one's *self respect* is adversely affected. To have our self respect diminished is to have suffered dehumanization. To be engaged in an association or activity which causes a person to reject or lose respect for himself is an intolerable situation. We *should* cross the line from tolerance to intolerance when our self respect would be diminished by doing something. No employer should want an employee to do anything so against the employee's conscience or sense of personal dignity that it would detract from his or her self respect. No employee should passively accept such assignments. An offended party has an ethical obligation to address the situation. The offending party has an ethical obligation to consider carefully the dignity of the threatened one. But neither party should be naive. Should differences of perception be very great, consequential adjustments of some type will be forthcoming. But people cannot afford to say, "My self respect is for sale. My life has a price." This would be unethical and dehumanizing, in itself.

Those who have reached the limits of their tolerance also have a need to be ethical in how they communicate with those above and around them about their discomfort. The offended party should follow the same principles that were set forth in the section dealing with the Ethics of Anger. The person that is bothered needs to state his or her sense of discomfort and the basis for it without attacking, putting down, criticizing, or impugning the character or intentions of the other parties. The differences of perception about what is right (and thus tolerable) need to be expressed but should not be used to attack others.

The consequences that can flow from such differences can be quite varied. The offending party could apologize and be careful not to offend the self respect of the other person in the future. The offended person may need to be transferred to an area where such expected activities are not required or they may simply not be asked to do certain things, which management deems ethical, while in that position. Or, differences may be so severe and deep as to necessitate a permanent separation from the organization. But under no condition should a superior ever ask a subordinate to do anything that the superior himself deems to be unethical beforehand. On the other side, a subordinate has a responsibility for communicating with the supervisor about any assignments that make him ethically uncomfortable. We cannot read each other's minds. We must communicate.

GROUP AIRING There are times when people can anticipate the unfolding of circumstances that will, in all probability result in their being put "between a rock and a hard place." If unethical pressure is anticipated, either from the circumstances or from those up the chain of command, getting the expected issues and situations "up on the table" before a group of decision makers will generally forestall any unethical consequences. When questionable ethical practices are openly discussed before a group of people, there are not many who will either suggest or imply that devious behavior should even be considered. If a group is capable of collectively agreeing upon immoral behavior, the person who is ethically sensitive is confronted with an entirely different type of problem at that point. Should the general moral level of a group allow for collective agreement upon unethical conduct, the individual who desires ethical decisions should know there is little hope of turning such a group to a moral course, unless their imprudence is demonstrably self-defeating.

A group that is routinely sound, however, even if not ethically committed on the conscious level, can be depended upon to keep an insensitive or unethical individual from determining the course of the group on touchy matters. If a sensitive and committed individual points out those ethical aspects that need to be considered, most people will want to do what is right. This is particularly true when their opinions are displayed before the group. Therefore, using a group as a means of establishing an ethical stance in a touchy situation is generally a good strategy.

If someone has already received an oral directive from a superior that requires action of an unethical nature, the recipient of the order should verbally communicate his *uneasiness* about the request. One may also politely ask that the directive be put in writing so that clear responsibility for its initiation can be established. But it must be remembered that any subordinate who carries out any directive also shares in the responsibility for it. Once a directive is given in private, it is inappropriate to bring it before a group without the initiator's consent. Should a subordinate not receive conscionable relief from an immediate superior, he should ask this person to please discuss it with his own superior. If refused, a true conflict has surfaced. The subordinate is in the weaker position authoritatively. A resolution of this kind of problem must first be sought by examining our personal level of acceptable tolerance and its impact upon our self respect. If these are violated, our ethics may well lead us in a direction where we should expect to "pay the price" for our convictions.

CONSISTENCY   People who are in a position of authority are exercising value judgments at almost every turn. Those who are affected by such judgments are also absorbing and/or evaluating their superior's exhibited values. Those in authority are not put there to please the people beneath them, but they are models to their subordinates. The unethical superior invites the exhibition of ignoble conduct on the part of his subordinates. The exhibition of hypocrisy, on the part of the leader, is a sure signal to those following him that ethics is a window dressing.

Those who would be ethical should want to exhibit a *consistency* in their conduct and decisions. Our pattern of conduct, over time, is crucial to developing respect. Things like trust, respect, and honor, that are long in building, are quick to dissipate if violated. There are both a time and a directional necessity for our ethical consistency. People must be consistent in their development and application of judgments or be very careful to explain and justify the apparent differences. Inconsistencies are frequently equated with our being unethical. Also, those who exercise authority will be closely watched to see if they treat those below them with less respect and courtesy than those above them. To be partial toward certain individuals is considered hypocritical and unethical by those experiencing the negative differences in a superior's behavior.

CONSIDERATION   Building people up is better than tearing
OF OTHERS   them down. Being kind to one another is
                  preferred over our being ugly. Harmony
is more desirable than chaos. Caring for the dignity and well being of others is a general principle that is completely compatible with self respect and self acceptance, which are essential to everyone's sense of well being. In fact, there can be no true self love or healthy egoism that is not considerate of the well being of others. Those philosophies that push concepts of egoism to the extremes of self-centeredness create the necessity for human isolation, feigned concern for others, or the denial of ethics as an appropriate reality. Ethics, as an expression of reality, is predicated upon the assumption that there are right and wrong motives, attitudes, traits of character, and actions that are exhibited in interpersonal relationships. Respectful social interaction is considered a norm by almost everyone.

If the above is true, then a pretense of considering others is un-ethical in itself. The acid test of this is not found in our logic or ability to discuss the matter, but it is realized in the fact that the overwhelming majority of people perceive others to be ethical when they observe what is considered to be their genuine kindness, consideration, politeness, empathy, and fairness in their interper-sonal relationships. When these are absent, and unkindness, incon-sideration, rudeness, hardness, and injustice are present, the people exhibiting such conduct are considered unethical. A genuine con-sideration of others is essential to an ethical life.

NEGATIVE ENABLING Being ethical does not imply pussyfooting around hard decisions or failing to con-front dehumanizing situations. Firmness and resoluteness are characteristics that are as harmonious with ethics as are consideration and kindness. When the carrying out of an appropriate action requires firmness, then it would be unethical to be otherwise. Being "right" and "good" are not to be auto-matically equated with being soft or popular, any more than they imply being hard or calloused. It means that we are to do what is right, even in the face of severe oppositon.

It is never fun to correct someone. It is a distasteful responsibility to have to share a poor evaluation with an employee. It is unpleasant to fire or release a worker. Yet, there are times when all of these are correct and ethical actions. What is the principle that needs to be kept in mind as one faces the responsibility of having to take hard and corrective actions? Managers, by their own decisions and actions, must not *enable* their workers to conduct themselves in a manner that is not conducive to their own or others' well being.

There is no self respect associated with poor work. If a person is incapable of doing a particular job satisfactorily, he is misplaced. Ethically, he needs to be removed and relocated in a job where he can perform well and develop his self esteem. A person who is capable of performing a task well, and does not, is in need of cor-rective action. Without it, he will not progress to the point of as-suming full responsibility for his own actions. To accept poor work is to enable a person to diminish his self respect by being al-lowed to do less than he is capable of doing. To enable a person to remain immature is unethical. To allow any conduct to continue that is not enhancing to the human dignity for everyone associated with an operation is to condone unethical behavior.

MUTUALLY
BENEFICIAL
In the economic arena there are many factors that interrelate which can result in the pairing of unequals in a transaction. Those who deal with each other may be unequal in knowledge, information, ability, financial strength, and other influential characteristics. The ethical question is, "To what degree can people capitalize on their advantage and still be considered ethical?" Or, put another way, "Is it unethical to capitalize on someone else's weaknesses?"

Taking advantage of another's ignorance or incompetency while conducting a transaction will generally be shortlived. The incompetent will get wise or cease to be able to afford their incompetency. The intentional seeking of advantages that exceed the benefits which would normally occur when competent parties interface with one another is indeed unethical. To purposefully seek the ignorant, incompetent, and weak is to look for benefits that are not attached to the transaction per se, but are a result of the deficiency of the individual carrying out the transaction. No human wants to be, or should be, the prey of another.

Therefore, those who desire what is right should not fall heir to the notion that in economic transactions there are "winners" and "losers." All economic transactions can and should be mutually beneficial. Transactional relationships that are mutually beneficial are enhancing to all parties. The enhancement of benefits is by definition salutary. It is good.

Unintended benefits and harms do at times result from or accompany, business transactions. The thrust of the above paragraphs is intended to address the transactional *motives* that make up all economic exchanges. It is simply not ethical to desire harm or loss for another person.

THE END
No human can require that anyone hold a particular set of ethics. No person can decide for another what is ethical. None are capable of convincing others that the "true truth" is to be found in a particular person or place. One person does not give

another a justification base upon which to decide what is ethical. However, none of this diminishes the importance of ethics. It can be said that a concept of "true truth" is importantly right while the others are importantly wrong (do not expect agreement on your choice, however), but it cannot be said that ethics is not important.

Ethics is the mirror of our civilization. Our personal ethics is the reflection of our own character. If our character is not important, then neither is life. And if life is not important, humans are the most pathetic portion of all existence. This would be true because our capacity for self awareness could be said to lead us to nonsense questions about our existence, meaning, and purpose. To be bothered with such concerns is indeed tragic, unless they speak to and point to the reality that humans do have meaning and purpose.

The author has a deep, personal commitment to the process of determining true truth. He also holds firm to a particular basis for his ethical justification. He believes life is full of meaning and purpose. He, therefore, believes it is good to be ethical. It builds people up and generates self respect. It builds trust and respect between people. It results in long-run benefits for all and is good in itself. The good tree produces good fruit. It produces harmony and peace. And yes, there are those who dislike ethically sensitive people in the same way boys set upon a prank do not want to be seen by anyone else. Ethical people can, and often do, make the unethical uncomfortable. But that is good for all, so long as good is better than bad and evil is something that ought to be overcome. Ethics requires no apology, only courage.

INDEX

F

facts, 29, 44, 47, 67, 80, 81, 117, 136, 141, 153, 165
  and values, 44, 45, 52, 55, 64, 65, 70, 115
  physical, 65, 66
fair, 54, 130, 166
fairness, 149, 176
fairs, 24
faith, 32, 33, 41, 45, 70, 82, 86, 94
  leap of, 45, 82, 106, 136
faithful, 69, 99
fall, 55, 108
  of man, 108
fallen, 81
false, 89, 115
fear, 25, 155
feelings, 3, 7, 11, 46, 60, 70, 91, 97, 106, 117, 132, 171
feet, 8, 13
flesh, 79
forces, 46, 67, 85, 116
forgiveness, 78, 79, 86
free, 22, 34, 139, 167
freedom, 20, 150, 164, 172
free will, 48, 108, 129
Friedman, Milton, 39
fruit, 22, 137
frustration, 155
future, 67, 154

G

Galilei, Galileo, 29
genesis, 2, 22, 23, 33, 96, 105, 153
genetics, 52, 130
genocide, 52, 139
gentleness, 132
goals, 67, 132
God, 11, 22, 29, 33, 34, 36, 47, 49, 51, 54, 55, 58, 61, 76-100, 133-140, 152, 164
  fellowship with, 108
  glorification of, 35
  image of, 101, 103
  /man view of reality, 40

  personal, 40
  sovereign, 41
golden rule, 131
good, 5, 7, 49, 52, 79, 99, 111-117, 121, 122, 130, 139, 140, 150, 176
  consequence, 111-125, 130, 139, 167
  in itself, 111-125, 139, 167
  intrinsic, 120
  lesser, 98, 99, 101, 107, 164, 165, 172
  works, 33
goodness, 130
government, 115, 132, 150, 154, 158, 163, 164
  regulations, 143, 160
grace, 34, 49
grail, ethical, 64
gratitude, 34, 79, 95
greed, 54, 64
grey, 145, 146
ground, common, 136, 137
group, 72, 92, 112, 131, 133, 135, 137, 157, 163, 165, 174
guidance, 46
guide, 4, 49, 50, 58, 61, 95, 111, 117, 144, 149
guilt, 20, 34
Gutenberg, Johann, 25

H

habit, 100
happiness, 104, 152, 157, 159
  illusory, 105
  true, 106
harm, 144, 147, 150, 159, 172
harmonize, 115
harmony, 17, 164, 175, 178
health, 54, 160
heart, 4, 55, 84, 87, 132, 144
  of God, 33, 79
heaven, 105
hedonism, 120
Hegel, G. W. F., 70, 97
Heilbroner, Robert, 25